P8-AUW-643

101 DISHES TO EAT BEFORE YOU DIE

101 DISHES TO EAT BEFORE YOU DIE

Stefan Gates

First published in 2009
Love Food ® is an imprint of Parragon Books Ltd

Parragon
Queen Street House
4 Queen Street
Bath, BA1 1HE, UK

Copyright © Parragon Books Ltd 2009

Love Food ® and the accompanying heart device is a trade mark of Parragon Books Ltd

All rights reserved. No part of this publication may be reproduced, stored in a retrieval system, or transmitted, in any form or by any means, electronic, mechanical, photocopying, recording, or otherwise, without the prior permission of the copyright holder.

ISBN: 978-1-4075-6255-1

Printed in Indonesia

Written by Stefan Gates
Project managed by Faye Lloyd
Edited by Fiona Biggs
Designed by Andrew Easton at Ummagumma
Photography by Mike Cooper
Food styling by Lincoln Jefferson

NOTES FOR THE READER

This book uses imperial, metric, and U.S. cup measurements. Follow the same units of measurement throughout; do not mix metric and imperial. All spoon measurements are level: teaspoons are assumed to be 5 ml, and tablespoons are assumed to be 15 ml. Unless otherwise stated, milk is assumed to be whole, eggs and individual vegetables are medium, and pepper is freshly ground black pepper.

The times given are an approximate guide only. Preparation times differ according to the techniques used by different people and the cooking times may also vary from those given. Optional ingredients, variations, or serving suggestions have not been included in the calculations.

Recipes using raw or very lightly cooked eggs should be avoided by infants, the elderly, pregnant women, convalescents, and anyone with a chronic condition. Pregnant and breastfeeding women are advised to avoid eating peanuts and peanut products. People with nut allergies should be aware that some of the prepared ingredients used in the recipes in this book may contain nuts. Always check the package before use.

PICTURE ACKNOWLEDGMENTS

The publisher would like to thank the following for permission to reproduce copyright material:
Corbis 191
Stock Food 70, 73, 173, 179, 253
Stefan Gates 9, 36, 41, 47, 115, 157, 158, 159, 161, 163, 165, 167, 169, 170, 175, 176, 177

Contents

Acknowledgments

Every food writer and chef on the planet would love the opportunity to write a book with such a breathtakingly, shockingly, incandescently arrogant title as *101 Dishes to Eat Before You Die*. I'd like to say a huge, big, hairy "thank you" to the wonderful Parragon ladies Vickie Voss and Faye Lloyd for letting me be the one to write it, and for their forbearance in allowing me to include some of the wilder and more wonderful dishes that might put a wimpier publisher off. Thanks also to Borra Garson, my agent, who keeps making it all happen.

The real food heroes of the world are the billions of ordinary cooks, the moms, dads, friends, and families who use food to express their love for each other on a daily basis, and who have discovered all the best parts of this book long before I ever did. That said, I could never properly thank all the brilliant authors, journalists, cooks, and chefs from whom I've absorbed, borrowed, and learned, so I'll just genuflect in the general direction of their glory. I still think that Jean-Anthelme Brillat-Savarin is the best of them all, despite the fact that his *Physiology of Taste* is somewhat lean on recipes. The man was a genius, and understood early on that food can be about adventure and wonder as much as a good meal.

A grand-scale, squealing, breathtaking cuddle goes to my girls Georgia, Daisy, and Poppy, who have definitely had a much better time than any others while I was writing this book. And finally, I'd like to dedicate this book to my Dad, Eric Gates, who, with an open, gentle, and ever-curious mind, has inspired me to try every food on the planet.

Truffles and Teargas

So, what are my credentials for deciding on such a crucial and contentious issue as the definitive list of 101 dishes to eat before you die? Well, it's a fair question. I guess I need to tell you a little bit about myself.

I have a strange and wonderful job that I enjoy so much it's almost embarrassing. Basically, I'm a food adventurer. If you think that sounds like an odd job title, then you're right, and I have no idea how I managed to turn a fascination for food into a job (believe me, if I knew, I'd tell you). As a small child I was obsessed with playing with my food, and the only toy I couldn't be parted from was a small and battered black saucepan, but I never in my wildest dreams imagined I'd make a living out of it. Now that I'm grown up, whenever the lovely people who make books and TV programs want someone to go off on culinary adventures and try to understand the world through the foods that people eat, they call me. I like to think I'm being paid to play with my food.

For my entire life I've been fascinated with the idea that food has a huge resonance beyond its function as fuel, and I wrote about it in a book called *Gastronaut*, which dealt with everything from gruel to gravlax, from cannibalism to the Last Supper. You see, food has form: it has emotional, cultural, and historical significance. It has been the root cause of wars, it's been used as a political, religious, and social tool, and it often defines societies. That fascinates me.

As well as cooking and writing about the best and tastiest foods on the planet, I also spend a fair amount of time making TV programs, such as *Cooking in the Danger Zone*, in which I travel the world, meeting people and finding out how they eat, cook, and survive in some of the most dangerous and difficult places on the earth. You'll be relieved to know that it's not just fun and indulgence: I've spent a fair amount of time in war zones and refugee camps, I've been smuggled over the Burmese border to live with Karen rebels in jungle camps, I've been shot at and tasted more teargas than I ever thought possible. And I've eaten a wider range of foods than anyone I know.

My search to find extraordinary food has taken me beyond the usual Michelin-starred truffle-touting restaurants and the great markets of Paris and Mexico to some of the strangest and most

difficult corners of the world. I've found myself tasting fresh goat blood in Ethiopia, radioactive borscht in Chernobyl, rotten walrus in the Arctic, mud cake in Haiti, yak's penis in China, sea slug intestines and cane rat in Cameroon. I've experimented with aftershave as an ingredient, tasted dog food and chicken feed, cooked gruel. Yesterday I cooked lamb's testicles lightly fried in garlic butter for a friend (fantastic, but not good enough to appear in this book) and, on a whim, I tried frying some earthworms from the garden (crunchy, but sadly flavorless).

What has this got to do with the 101 dishes to eat before you die? Well, it's all about a sense of context. I reckoned that I needed to eat the worst, the weirdest, and the most wonderful foods on the earth in order to come up with a credible list of the most important.

So my list of 101 dishes doesn't just include the tastiest dishes on the planet, although the great majority are. Some are included because they are a little piece of theater ("Spectacular"), or the summation of centuries of cultural history ("International"), or because they are amazing, life-affirming expressions of love and nutrition ("Comfort"). Some of them (I like to think that they are the best of all) are here because they are extraordinary, surprising, or simply unforgettable.

Stefan

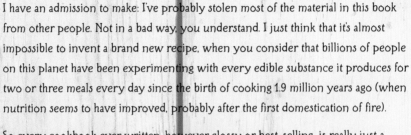

What's in this book?

I have an admission to make: I've probably stolen most of the material in this book from other people. Not in a bad way, you understand. I just think that it's almost impossible to invent a brand new recipe, when you consider that billions of people on this planet have been experimenting with every edible substance it produces for two or three meals every day since the birth of cooking 1.9 million years ago (when nutrition seems to have improved, probably after the first domestication of fire).

So every cookbook ever written, however glossy or best-selling, is really just a compilation of all the best work from the most brilliant cooks, farmers, alchemists, writers, and eaters since the birth of cooking. I know that we food writers refine, rewrite, recipe test, and edit; we try to be original and inspiring and to inject a sense of relevance and context, but really we are rewriting the best material of our ancestors. I think that this is a good thing.

This book simply draws a line in the shifting sands of global cuisine, picking 101 dishes that I think you really should try before you die, giving you my personal justification for choosing each dish and offering you as much information about it as I could fit into the space. I see food as a route to enlightenment and excitement—an adventure that you can have in the safety of your own kitchen—and I also like my meals to have a story to them.

101 Dishes to Eat Before You Die is in many ways an anthology of great food and, as with an anthology of great poetry, you are likely to appreciate the sensual journey so much more when you understand its background, history, and the quirky route through which it came to fruition. I hope that the extra information I've given will help you to really understand and enjoy these dishes.

The food that I've chosen to write about in this book is rarely the most refined or perfectly presented. Other than those included in the chapter entitled "Expensive," there are few recipes that are too expensive for everyday eating, and few recipes that require much more than basic kitchen skills and a passion for food. I'm not much of a fan of making Michelin-starred-type food in domestic kitchens—I rarely have the equipment or the audience to appreciate gels, millefeuilles, spun sugar, and minute portions. Very occasionally, however, I eat the odd bouffanted, fancy, three-starred meal, and I do enjoy them immensely. If you want to blow a king's ransom just once in your life on the finest foods any restaurant has to offer, make your way to Heston Blumenthal's Fat Duck in Bray, just outside London, England, for a sensual and culinary journey like no other. Heston's food is transcendentally good, it's dramatic (like his liquid-nitrogen-poached green tea mousse) and even funny (smoked salmon and scrambled egg ice cream). But no Fat Duck-esque dishes appear here.

This book is intended to be the opposite of all that: it's approachable and cook-friendly, yet at the same time extraordinary and inspirational. It's not hard to hit this balance when so many of the best dishes on the earth are so absurdly simple that they hardly rate as recipes: toro tuna, shrimp in garlic butter, crab, fruits de mer, Pata Negra ham, ceviche, tapenade, and cheese. Their glory is often due to the love and care shown to the ingredients by fishermen, farmers, and cheesemakers.

I happily hold my hands up and admit that the chapters that are closest to my heart are "Perfect," which lists my ten personal favorite dishes because they excite and calm me like no others can; and "Spectacular," which contains my favorite interactive, dramatic, or collaborative foods, and that I love for the fun and sheer exhilaration of the eating experience.

I know that there is a handful of recipes (mainly in the "Wild" chapter) that very few of you will ever try, often because they are hard to source or just plain terrifying. I just hope that by telling you about some of them, it might encourage you to be a little bit more adventurous at home in your own kitchen.

But, everyone is different, and, when it comes to food, as with anything else, we all have our likes, dislikes, and prejudices, and any list of 101 dishes to eat before you die is likely to cause arguments. If you think that I've made any terrible omissions or, indeed, if you really think you've invented a brand new recipe that no one else has tried in 1.9 million years, feel free to drop me a line and I'll take a look. Watch out though: I might drop in with my knife and fork, asking for proof!

1. Perfect

Perfect

These are, simply, the ten dishes I love above all others. My perfect 10. If you boiled all these down and dug them into your flower border, you would come back a few days later to find a little me growing in your yard, wondering what's for lunch. But the root causes of my love for these dishes are a nebulous miscellany of magical, emotional, or personal reasons that are hard to pigeonhole, which is why I've used the fluffy, conceptual superlative "Perfect" to group them together.

Put simply, these are the foods that make me the person I am, starting with my all-time favorite meal: Beef Carpaccio. I usually make this the day after I've flown back home from working somewhere remote, dangerous, or distressing. It's a way of rediscovering myself and returning to all the things I love, and I usually make it calmly, slowly, and deliberately, alone and quiet in my kitchen, warm in the knowledge that my wife will be joining me later to share it. It's like a benediction, a warm hug of approval. Sorry if that sounds wet and sentimental, but I'm sure you also have meals that summon up feelings from unfathomable depths. That's what I love about food: its power to express deep, primal emotions.

To talk in less fluffy terms, some of the dishes here are "Perfect" because they are so well balanced. My love for Figs & Young Goat Cheese and Roasted Red Bell Pepper Salad comes from my memories of making them for friends in the south of France, but they are also extraordinary combinations. Scallops and Pea Puree is possibly the nearest to a perfect combination of textures and flavors that I have ever eaten, a journey of sensory pleasure that I love so much it sometimes brings tears to my eyes when I eat it. There I go again, getting all emotional. But don't laugh: it's true!

Some of these dishes are here because they are life-enhancing spectacles that have been the seed of so much pleasure and laughter that it would be criminal not to include them. Crab & Stone Party is one of these. It's a way of turning a meal into a celebration and a riot at the same time. Fruits de Mer will always be thought of as a romantic dish, and I don't think I've ever eaten it without feeling like I'm in a movie, on the verge of something wonderful (and a little mischievous).

Roast Pork Spareribs is a life-affirming food that makes me happy for simple reasons: it's uncomplicated, cheap, and easy to make, yet it's also spectacular and tastes so unbelievably good. It's a wonderful party food because you can make it easily on a huge scale without mortgaging your grandma, and my kids love the bone-gnawing that they are allowed to do with the ribs. Tokyo Sushi is here simply because I eat so much of it that it would be criminal to exclude it.

I realize that food and personal experience is subjective and relative, and that one guy's "Perfect" is often another gal's "Whatever," but I truly believe that all of these dishes will make your life brighter and happier.

① Beef Carpaccio

There's no point being shy about this: Beef Carpaccio is my favourite dish of all time. Eating it makes me think that everything's all right with the world. I spend a fair proportion of my time working in the planet's more dangerous and difficult places, discovering strange, wonderful, but often unsettling foods, and I eat this marinated raw beef dish the moment I get back because it's the opposite of all that: it's refined, unashamedly expensive, balanced, and delicate. This is what cows were made for.

You need to buy the very best well-hung beef tenderloin or sirloin that you can afford, and it's always a good idea to mention to your butcher that you'll be eating it as raw carpaccio. If he's anything like my butcher, his eyes will light up, and he'll search for a particularly fantastic specimen—you are, by eating his best meat raw, showing the ultimate appreciation of his skills and integrity.

Oddly enough, this is a dish that restaurants never seem to be able to get right. It's invariably disappointing because most restaurants simply freeze the beef, then cut it so thin that it's almost transparent. Please don't do that. Instead, firm the meat up for a short while in the freezer, cut it fairly thinly, then squash it flat with the blade of a flat knife, tenderizing it but keeping the texture.

The word "carpaccio" has become shorthand for any food offered raw and thinly sliced (such as swordfish or pineapple—see page 245), but it originally referred to the deep red colors used by Venetian Renaissance painter Vittore Carpaccio. It was invented at the famous Harry's Bar in Venice, Italy, where they serve it with a lemony mayonnaise, although this version is so much better.

Vittore Carpaccio

Vittore Carpaccio was a great, if relatively neglected painter of the early Venetian school, who lived from 1460 to 1525/6. He did, indeed, paint with a lot of red, although much of it has now faded to a pallid pink. One exception is his Vision of St. Augustine, which still beams shocking, livid, almost rude vermilion at the viewer.

ingredients

Serves 6 as a rich appetizer

1 lb 2 oz/500 g beef tenderloin, cut from the thin end

generous ³/₄ cup extra virgin olive oil

¹/₄ cup pine nuts

7 oz/200 g arugula

1 oz/25 g Parmesan cheese

2 tsp truffle oil

salt and pepper

crusty bread, to serve

**To drink:
A very pale
rosé wine**

method

Put the beef in the freezer for an hour before use to firm it up for easier cutting. Trim any fat or sinew from the beef, then cut it into slices as thin as you can manage.

Lay a slice of beef on a cutting board and, using a flat, broad knife, press against the meat, pushing down hard and pulling toward you in a spreading motion several times across each slice, trying not to tear it too much. As well as making the meat thin, this will tenderize it. Repeat with all the beef slices.

Pour a little pool of olive oil into a wide dish. Place a layer of beef on the oil, season lightly with salt and pepper, and pour over some more oil. Repeat until all the beef has been seasoned in this way. Cover the dish with plastic wrap and let chill in the refrigerator for 30 minutes to 2 hours. Heat the pine nuts in a dry skillet over medium heat, until lightly toasted, and set aside.

When you're ready to eat, lay a bed of arugula on each of six serving plates, then remove the beef slices from the marinade and divide evenly between the plates. Scatter with the pine nuts and shave the Parmesan cheese over, using a vegetable peeler. Lay a few extra leaves of arugula on top of each plate, drizzle over a few drops of truffle oil, and serve with bread.

② Scallops & pea puree

This is a rare and beautiful balance of textures and flavors. Pan-seared scallops have a wondrous, lightly caramelized crispness on the outside, a rude silky smoothness on the inside, and are served on a bed of pea puree that's clean, simple, and pure. It's a marriage made in heaven and it looks fantastic. Yet, despite this, it's absurdly easy to make, which makes it all the more extraordinary.

Scallops are one of those ingredients like crab and lobster that taste light and clean, but are actually beguilingly filling. Buy the biggest, freshest, and fattest that you can find, but don't be tempted to serve too many to each person, otherwise you'll lose the magic. Less is more.

While you shouldn't be tempted to make this dish complicated, it would be criminal of me not to mention that you could add one extra element: a slice of fried blood sausage underneath each scallop. Sounds weird, doesn't it? Blood sausage seems such a rough, boisterous ingredient. And yet something strange and magical happens when you marry it with the purity of the scallop—like Richard Gere and Julia Roberts in *Pretty Woman*, or Rex Harrison and Audrey Hepburn in *My Fair Lady*, some matches were just meant to be.

Did you know that scallops can swim?

Yup, I've seen it with my own eyes. When you disturb them from the seabed they move with extraordinary speed (well, extraordinary for a bivalve!) by opening and closing their shells very fast to propel them up and away. They use their adductor muscle—the part that we find so delicious—and because of this extraordinary ability, they are the only migratory bivalve.

I wondered if the scallop knew where it was going when it set off on its panicky swim, but it turns out that they have a lot of complex little eyes with retinas around their rims—although they are always looking backward while on the move. In fact, most bivalves can sense shadows falling across them, but few are as developed as the scallop. They are also hermaphrodites, but that's a whole different story.

ingredients

Serves 4 as a main course (a perfect size if you've served an appetizer). By the way, the method of frying the scallops may seem a little odd, but trust me—it's fantastic.

4 1/2 cups frozen peas

2 large handfuls fresh mint leaves, roughly chopped

3/4 cup butter

12 fat scallops, roes attached, if possible, and removed from their shells

salt and pepper

olive oil, for drizzling

method

Bring a large saucepan of water to a boil, then add the peas. Return to a boil and simmer for 3 minutes. Drain the peas, then put them in a food processor with the mint, two thirds of the butter, and a large pinch of salt. Blend to a smooth puree, adding a little hot water if the mixture needs loosening. Taste for seasoning, cover, and keep warm.

Pat the scallops dry, then season them well with salt and pepper. Melt the remaining butter in a large skillet over high heat. When the butter starts to smoke, add the scallops and sear them for 1–2 minutes on each side (don't be tempted to cook them for longer!). They should be brown and crisp on the outside but light and moist in the middle. Remove the skillet from the heat.

Spread a pool of pea puree on each of four warmed plates, and place the scallops on top. Drizzle over a little olive oil, season, and serve.

To drink: A solid white Burgundy

③ Tokyo sushi

Fish fascinates me in the same way that fine art fascinates others. Some people never forget the day they saw their first Canaletto, Rothko, or Turner, but my seminal visual moment was walking into a fish dealer's where an entire basket of small live spider crabs had escaped over a display of the most exquisite fresh fish.

I often drop into my local fish dealer and buy one of everything that looks sparkling fresh (or as many as I can afford). I take the fish home, luxuriate in the cleaning and filleting; and then simply lay them on white servers and serve them with a bowl of sushi rice.

I used to think that this was just my uniquely slapdash way of eating sashimi, but when I visited Tokyo I discovered that the Japanese often eat it like this. You don't have to make maki rolls and nigiri fingers to enjoy the transcendental delights of fine, super-fresh, raw fish. You do, however, need to be careful that the fish really is the finest quality (and often, that doesn't come cheap). One note of caution though: Never refrigerate sushi rice once it has been cooked—it will lose all of that wonderful texture. Serve at room temperature.

The best fish for sushi:

Mackerel is a wonderful sushi fish, one of my favorites. However, make sure it's extremely fresh and is neither too large nor too small, otherwise it will be very difficult to remove the pin bones. I recommend scallops (sounds strange, I know, but they are mind-blowingly good), mackerel (super cheap and high in oils), salmon, sea bass, and red snapper.

ingredients

Serves 4 as a main course

1¹/₂ cups sushi rice

1 credit-card-size piece of konbu seaweed (optional)

1 lb 12 oz/800 g selection of superbly fresh fish fillets, such as wild salmon, scallops, sea bass, mackerel, red snapper, or fantastic tuna (ask your fish dealer to fillet, skin, and bone them for sushi)

4 fat scallops, roes attached

4 tbsp rice vinegar

2 tbsp sugar

1 tsp salt

To serve
prepared wasabi
light soy sauce
ponzu (optional)

method

Wash the rice in a bowl of cold water, but do it very gently, massaging the grains in the water with your fingers, otherwise they will break up. Keep changing the water until it runs clear, then cook (together with the konbu, if using) according to the package instructions, using a rice cooker if you have one. Let the rice cool until just warm to the touch, then remove and discard the konbu (the cooking and cooling will take around 60 minutes in total).

Meanwhile, prepare the fish. Remove any remaining pin bones using fish tweezers or a pair of small pliers. It's worth taking your time with this. Cut across the grain of the flesh to make slices half the width of your pinkie. Cut the scallops into three or four round slices. Cover and set aside.

Combine the rice vinegar, sugar, and salt in a small saucepan and place over very low heat. Stir until the sugar has dissolved. Fold this into the rice very gently with a wooden spoon, using a cutting motion.

Place some rice in four wide, shallow bowls, then lay a selection of the raw fish on top. Serve with wasabi, soy sauce, and ponzu, if using, in separate bowls.

To drink: Japanese Asahi super-dry beer

④ Roast pork spareribs

Lamb flaps

In Tonga there's a strong tradition of eating lamb flaps—the term they use to describe lamb belly. It's an interesting dish that I have rarely seen around the rest of the world, which is a shame because it's delicious, although it is extraordinarily fatty. In fact, the Tongans' love of flaps is one of the reasons that they have one of the highest levels of obesity in the world. Although they do also eat a vast amount of suckling pig, coconut milk, and corned beef soup (oh yes). If you lay your hands on lamb flaps, try them, but don't eat them every day or you'll be on your way to some seriously bad health.

Just writing the words "roast pork spareribs" makes me want to rush to the butcher and sign over my worldly possessions to him (or at least all those possessions I haven't already signed over to him). This is one of those ultimate feasts that I'd choose to eat as my last meal on the earth, for these reasons:

1. It's pants-shakingly, head-burstingly, palate-bustingly delicious, it's succulent, and it's covered in the most magical edible substance on the planet: pork cracklings.

2. It's spectacular to serve—a grand-scale hunk of Fred Flintstone-esque carnivorality that hits the table with a wallop and physically oozes goodness. The cook cuts the ribs into hunks that the diner gnaws on like a medieval English monarch—knives and forks are useless here—and everyone makes a mess of their shirts.

3. It's very cheap.

4. It's virtually indestructible—even the most scatterbrained and under-equipped cook can make this.

5. How many more reasons do you need? Go make it! Quick!

You need to buy a whole, well-raised, unadulterated hunk of spareribs, bones still in, and skin still on, but ask for the skin to be scored. If the butcher doesn't do this for you, you'll need to do it yourself with a very sharp knife.

It's best to marinate this for a few hours or overnight, although I've sometimes been in such a frenzy of porky excitement that I've thrown the marinade over it and slammed it straight in the oven. It doesn't really do justice to the dish, but it's possible.

ingredients

Serves 8

15 dried bay leaves

5 x 1-inch/2.5-cm pieces
fresh ginger, grated

15 garlic cloves, peeled and roughly chopped

generous $^1/_3$ cup olive oil

$^1/_2$ tsp pepper

2 tsp salt

1 tbsp whole cardamom seeds, cracked
(optional)

6 lb 8 oz/3 kg pork spareribs, complete with
skin and bones (make sure there are 8 ribs),
skin scored with a knife about
every $^1/_2$ inch/1 cm

Roast Potatoes (see page 113) and glazed
carrots, to serve

method

Combine all of the ingredients, except the pork, in a
small food processor, or mash using a large pestle and
mortar, until a thick paste forms. Put the pork spareribs
into a roasting pan that will fit in your refrigerator,
then rub the paste into it on all sides, making sure you
get some into the cuts through the fat. Now put it in
the refrigerator for at least 1 hour and up to 2 days.

Preheat the oven to 325°F/160°C. Place the pork,
uncovered, in the oven and roast for 2 hours.
Increase the oven temperature to 475°F/240°C and
cook for an additional 20–30 minutes to crisp the
skin, checking every 10 minutes to make sure that
the pork doesn't burn.

If the pork skin hasn't turned into good cracklings
by now, heat the broiler to high and place the pork
under the broiler, making sure that it doesn't burn.
Cut off the cracklings in one large piece and set aside,
uncovered. Cover the meat with foil and let rest for
15 minutes before serving. Cut it at the table, giving
each person a whole rib and a chunk of cracklings.

To drink: Vacqueyras red wine
from the French Rhône

⑤ Figs & young goat cheese

This beautiful combination of plump, ripe fruit and soft, heady goat cheese is one of the finest ways to end an open-air midsummer meal. Obviously, the meal is best eaten on a terrace overlooking vineyards that stretch across the land until they give way to a lagoon bursting with oyster beds. But if all you have is a balcony, an open window, or even just a postcard of your dream getaway stuck to the wall, this dish will fill in the gaps.

I know what you're thinking: "That's not a dish. It's a couple of ingredients on a cutting board." And you're right. But the combination of these two foods is one that was made in heaven.

You obviously need to choose the right ingredients; otherwise you'll wonder what all the fuss was about. The figs should be the big, plump, first-crop summer fruit that look as if they are about to burst. Tickle them before you buy them—they should feel heavy and fat, and fragrant under your nose. The goat cheese should be soft, but not overpoweringly goaty. The important thing is to try a lot before you buy. I always think that if I don't feel full when I leave the cheese counter, I've been shortchanged.

Picking figs

In the Languedoc region of the south of France, fig trees often have two harvests: a huge, early one that produces vast, tender fruit bursting with flavor, and a second, more disappointing one that produces, small, less fragrant figs.

1. Pick early in the day when it's not too hot.
2. Cover every inch of yourself before you pick. The leaves of the tree can be extremely irritating to the skin.
3. Don't leave the figs on the tree too late into the season, otherwise you'll miss the opportunity and they will attract every wasp in the area. If you have to pick more than you can eat fresh, they make unbelievably good preserves.
4. Ask someone to stand on the bottom rung of your ladder. You will be tempted to go higher than you should, and if your companion doesn't save you from mortal peril, at least he will have witnessed your bravery while gathering his lunch.

ingredients

Serves 6 as an appetizer or a dessert

12 fat, ripe figs
10 $\frac{1}{2}$ oz/300 g full-flavored soft
goat cheese
fragrant honey, for drizzling

method

Take the cheese and the figs out of the refrigerator an hour before you intend to eat them.

Cut the stalky top off the figs, then cut a cross into each fruit, most of the way to the bottom. Squeeze the sides of the figs to open them up. Place two figs on each plate. Put a slice of the goat cheese next to the fruit, then drizzle a generous spoonful of honey over the figs and the cheese. That's it!

To drink: La Baume Syrah rosé from the Languedoc, southern France

⑥ Roasted red bell pepper salad

I know, I know. A salad doesn't sound like the most exciting dish. But bear with me, because this little baby is the sexiest salad ever. It's rich, deeply flavored, and it deserves to be in the "Perfect" chapter because all the ingredients are powerful and pungent, but still work together beautifully.

Red bell peppers are one of those beguiling ingredients that are pleasant enough—nice even—when raw, but are transformed phoenixlike by fire into sweet, unctuous powerhouses of flavor. It's essential to broil or grill them until the skin blackens so that you can peel them easily.

Incidentally, if you're tempted to use green bell peppers because they're available, they're cheap, and surely they can't taste that different from the red ones, STOP RIGHT THERE! They are like slightly bitter cardboard in comparison to the real thing. There's only one place for a green bell pepper, and that's sitting quietly on the Capsicum annuum plant, waiting to ripen, sweeten, and turn red. Okay, I'll concede that history dictates that jambalaya and some paellas need green bell peppers, but that's really it.

The recipe calls for you to separate the yolk and white of the egg yet still serve them in the same dish. Now, I know that this sounds a bit ridiculous, but it makes a huge difference. I can't explain why, but trust me: I've tried cheating this, and it's not worth it.

This is an appetizer, but it's extremely rich, so don't be tempted to pile loads of it onto your plate, or you'll have no room left for your main course. And another thing: Although this recipe doesn't take a lot of work, the broiling is time-consuming. To make your life easier, you can prepare the bell peppers up to two days in advance.

ingredients

Serves 6 as a rich appetizer

2 lb 4 oz/1 kg very large red bell peppers

2 hard-cooked eggs

12 canned anchovies, rinsed and drained

1 tbsp capers, rinsed

1 large handful fresh basil leaves

1 tbsp chopped parsley

generous ¹/₃ cup olive oil

2 tbsp red wine vinegar

salt and pepper

good crusty bread, to serve

method

Preheat the broiler to high, then put the whole bell peppers into a roasting pan and place them under the heat. The skin will slowly start to blacken and loosen. Turn them before they burn too much—every 5 or 10 minutes. They will take 20–40 minutes to blacken, depending on their size. When they are black all over, put them in a saucepan with a lid on to let cool (this makes them sweat and helps the skins to loosen). When cool enough to handle, cut them open and remove the stalks and seeds. Peel them carefully, teasing the skin away from the valuable flesh, and reserving the juices. Cut the flesh into slices two fingers thick and arrange on a large serving plate.

Shell the eggs and cut them in half. Separate the yolks and the whites, then finely chop or grate the whites into one bowl and pass the yolks through a strainer into another bowl. Place 12 small piles of egg white on the serving plate at regular intervals.

Top the piles with anchovy fillets, and then egg yolk. Scatter the rinsed capers and herbs over, and pour over the oil, vinegar, and any juices you managed to save from the bell peppers. Season well with salt and pepper and serve with crusty bread.

To drink: Alsatian Gewürztraminer

⑦ Crab & stone party

This dish is a paradox: On one side you've got the tender, delicate, complex flavor of fresh crab, and on the other, you've got the sheer primal scream of smashing it apart with a rock. If it weren't for the fact that this tastes delicious, you'd be paying me for anger management therapy!

Each person is given a crab and an apron (things will be messy), a stone, and a cutting board for breaking the shell apart and extracting its magical fluffy, fibrous flesh. If you don't have any clean stones at your disposal, then you could use mallets or hammers. I recently served this to a group of friends and asked them all to bring along a clean hammer. They thought they were coming over to help me put up some shelves!

I'm fond of making food fun and interactive. It's not silliness or flippancy that I enjoy, but the uplifting sensory experience of really getting to grips with your food, and I swear that it makes the food taste better. Also, meals like this break down barriers between people and make for lots of love and laughter.

P. S. Don't throw away the shells and shreds— keep them to make the bisque on page 100.

Crabs for virgins

Here's what to do with your crab and stone:

Once the crabs are cooked and cooled, pull off all the legs and claws and set them aside for picking.

Pull the undercarriage section from the main body of the crab (if this is difficult, place the main body on its edge on the table with the eyes downward, then whack the back of the undercarrriage with the bottom of your palm until it dislodges). Discard anything plasticky-looking and the "dead men's fingers," or stringy gills. Everything else is edible, and there's a lot of wonderful stuff tucked away in the leg casing—getting to it is all part of the fun. There's lots of meat of various colors in the main shell. Some people are put off by the dark meat, so save it for making crab linguini (mix it with lime juice, chile, garlic, parsley, and loads of olive oil, and toss it in cooked pasta).

The best white meat is in the claws and legs—crack them open and tease it out with the handle of a teaspoon.

method

You'll need a stone and a cutting board for each person. If you have bought live crabs, you'll need to boil them first. Bring a large saucepan of heavily-salted water to a boil. Drop in the crabs, cover with a lid, and return to a boil. After it reaches boiling point, crabs up to 2 lb 2 oz/1 kg in weight will need 10–12 minutes to cook, 4 lb 4 oz/2 kg crabs will need 18 minutes.

Remove from the heat and drain carefully. Let the crabs cool before serving, remembering to cover them if you have a cat in the house!

Ingredients

1 crab per person—either freshly cooked or live

Mayonnaise (see page 67)

salad and bread and butter, to serve

To drink:
Bone-dry Picpoul de Pinet from the Languedoc, southern France

⑧ Baby fava beans & chorizo

Baby fava beans are extraordinarily tender, sweet, and delicious, and shelling them is very therapeutic. It's one of those lovely tasks that my children love helping with, or that I will happily go through at the kitchen table, especially when aided by a plate of cured meat, a glass of dry Oloroso sherry, and a radio. Actually, given that trio, I could happily do any manual task for days on end without getting bored, including the much more intricate task of mature fava bean skinning (see below).

If you're using fresh fava beans, this is a spring dish and you should shell and use the beans as soon as possible, before the sugar in them turns to starch. However, if you find frozen baby fava beans in the stores, slip them into your freezer and you'll be able to enjoy this at any time of the year! It's beautifully balanced, with the young, tender, delicate beans mixed together with the bullying, spicy chorizo—the crunch of spring vegetable juxtaposed with the mouthwatering luxury of juicy sausage. Oh, and this can also be made very successfully with young green peas.

Fava bean skinning

Older fava beans have a thick skin that children often hate and even for adults can be a bit tasteless. However, if you have a bit of time, even these can be transformed into a sublime ingredient. Simply nick the skin of the bean with your fingernail and squeeze the bean out. It's fussy work, but not difficult.

The fava bean

This is one of the original staple foods of Europe, and was overtaken by the cannellini bean in popularity only after the latter was imported during the Columbian Exchange of the late fifteenth and early sixteenth centuries.

If you visit a Spanish deli you might find little bags of what look like pale yellow dry-roasted fava beans. They don't look particularly appealing, to tell you the truth, but you should grab some anyway—they have been dried and roasted, often in a generous dredging of salt, and they are a fantastic little snack. They are especially good with beer, for some reason.

method

Place a heavy-bottom skillet over medium heat and add the olive oil. When it's shimmering hot, add the chorizo and brown it on all sides for about 15 minutes. Remove it from the skillet and set aside. Reduce the heat, add the scallions and garlic, and fry for an additional 5 minutes. Add the stock and fava beans and simmer for 3–5 minutes, until the beans are just tender. Add the mint and the cooked chorizo, stir through, and season with salt and pepper. Serve, with the juices, on small warmed plates, with some sourdough toast on the side.

ingredients

Serves 4 as an appetizer

1 tbsp olive oil
9 oz/250 g fresh chorizo sausage, chopped into finger-thick circles.
4 scallions, sliced
3 garlic cloves, crushed
generous $1/3$ cup chicken stock or vegetable stock, warmed
4 lb 4 oz/2 kg young fava beans in their pods, or about 1 lb 10 oz/750 g shelled frozen baby fava beans
1 large handful fresh mint, chopped
salt and pepper
toasted sourdough bread, to serve

To drink: Either La Gitana Manzanilla sherry or, if you can find it, a spectacular Pasada Pastrana sherry

⑨ Spectacular fruits de mer

This is easily the sexiest dish on the planet. There's something deliciously exhilarating, indulgent, and decadent about diving into a plate of spanking fresh shellfish nestled on shards of crisp crushed ice. Perhaps it's all that zinc in the oysters, perhaps it's the delectable range of textures, the exquisite flavors, and the outrageous sensory carnival of the whole thing. But there's also a frisson of excitement from the fact that it's so often washed down with Champagne, frequently eaten while on vacation, and with the diners dressed in their most glamorous clothes and jewelry. Let's face it, when you see a plateau de fruits de mer on the table in a big blockbuster movie, it's a sign that the lead actors will soon be getting down to some heavy making out at the very least.

Now, I can't deny that this dish needs a little more care, attention, and cash than many meals, but the sheer excitement and drama of serving something like this makes it all thoroughly worth while, whether it's for a romantic night in with your partner (or someone you'd like to be your partner), or served as a huge treat to a group of your best, most deserving friends. The up-side is that even if it's more expensive than the average dinner, preparing it will still cost a fraction of the price charged by most restaurants.

Strictly speaking, fruits de mer covers anything that lives in the sea and is edible—other than fish. Your collection of crustaceans and mollusks can include anything you like but I'd go for a base layer of the more approachable cooked varieties, such as crab, lobster, and big shrimp, so that any wimps at the table are catered for. Then you can go to town on the raw and more adventurous species—for my money, a good spread of oysters is essential, and then snails, clams, and mussels (you can lightly steam the last two, but they are often eaten raw in France). The real fun is in the more unusual varieties such as razor clams and sea urchins [see page 190].

Top tip
Don't forget to make or buy lots of ice in advance! You'll also need some nutcrackers, crab pliers, or hammers to share.

ingredients

a maximum of 1 lb 10 oz/750 g shellfish
per person, from the following list :

lobster, cooked

crab, cooked

oysters

large shrimp, cooked

mussels

clams

sea snails, cooked

razor clams

periwinkles, cooked

sea urchins

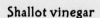

Shallot vinegar

1 shallot

4 tbsp red wine vinegar

To serve

crusty French baguette

Mayonnaise (see page 67)

lemon wedges

Tabasco sauce

method

Create a bed of crushed ice by taking a few handfuls of ice cubes at a time and placing them in a dish towel that isn't too cherished. Beat them with a rolling pin, mallet, or hammer until they have been crushed to a rough, gravely consistency. Keep in the freezer.

To make the shallot vinegar, finely chop the shallot and mix with the vinegar in a small bowl.

Lay a bed of crushed ice on a large serving plate, then make a centerpiece, using the lobster cut in half and the crab with the shell cracked ready for eating (see page 28). The oysters should surround the centerpiece, interspersed with the shrimp (in their whole shells), mussels, and clams, and the other bivalves scattered wherever they can fit (usually served in the shell they are attached to).

Serve with the shallot vinegar, sliced baguette, mayonnaise in small bowls, lemon wedges, and Tabasco sauce. Put a large bowl on the table for the discarded shells.

To drink: A fine bone-dry Champagne

⑩ French onion tart

Onion tart is a simple dish made from cheap ingredients, but when cooked with love and care it can be as sweet and pure as any haute cuisine flight of fancy. It is, in many ways, a perfect expression of the cook's art alongside dishes such as soufflé, risotto, and crème brulée—all recipes whose main figurative ingredient is patience.

The patisseries that sell prepared onion tarts are still a central part of French life, and this makes me a very happy man. In my favorite Languedoc village, there are two patisseries (both fantastic, although my allegiance is firmly with the Pain d'Or and its flirtatious Madame). Each has to get a mayoral declaration to close for its vacation, and this is granted only on the proviso that the other patisserie has the capacity to cope on its own. Sometimes you just have to throw your hands up in the air and say "I LOVE the French!"

How to stop onions making you cry

The volatile substance allicin is to blame for making us cry when we cut onions, and a fair amount of human endeavor has been expended trying to solve this problem. I admit that I get particularly badly affected—some medium-size ones have been known to put me out of action for an hour. I have even experimented with wearing construction safety goggles, which, bizarrely, doesn't work. The only way I've really managed to stop crying is to wear a half-face diving mask with a long snorkel, but it terrifies my kids, so I've resolved to just cry and bear it. Other methods include cutting them under running water (this has the unfortunate side effect of making you chop your fingertips off) and chilling them in the freezer before cutting.

The onion

The allium has been around since prehistoric times, and is central to most cuisines. The Egyptians were big fans, and they painted and wrote about them as well as cooking with them, although their priests were forbidden to eat them. Onions are taboo for some people, including the Hindu Brahmins and adherents of Jainism, who avoid all root vegetables.

method

First, make the pie dough. Sift the flour and salt together into a large bowl, add the butter, then rub with your fingers until grainy. Add the egg yolk and just enough of the water until the mixture holds together. Roll into a ball, wrap in plastic wrap, and let chill in the refrigerator for 15 minutes before using.

Preheat the oven to 350°F/180°C. Press the pastry into an 8-inch/20-cm loose-bottom tart pan, lay a piece of wax paper on it, cover with dried beans, and bake in the preheated oven for 15 minutes. Remove from the oven and increase the oven temperature to 400°F/200°C. Remove the beans and paper and bake the pastry shell for an additional 5 minutes.

To make the filling, melt the butter in a large, heavy-bottom skillet over low–medium heat, then add the onions and thyme and fry gently, stirring frequently until lightly browned. This will take 15–30 minutes. Season with salt and pepper, remove from the heat, and let cool for 10 minutes.

Preheat the oven to 375°F/190°C. In a large bowl, beat the eggs and cream together. Add the cheese, nutmeg, and cooked onions and mix in. Pour the mixture into the pastry shell and bake, uncovered, for 30–40 minutes, until golden brown (check after 20 minutes to make sure it's not burning). Serve the tart warm.

ingredients

Serves 6 as a main course

Pie dough

scant 1^1/$_2$ cups all-purpose flour

pinch of salt

3^1/$_2$ tbsp unsalted butter, diced

1 egg yolk

1 tbsp cold water

Filling

6 tbsp butter

4 onions, peeled and thinly sliced

2 tsp thyme leaves

2 eggs

1 cup heavy cream

scant ^{1}/$_2$ cup grated Gruyère cheese

^{1}/$_2$ tsp freshly-grated nutmeg

salt and pepper

To drink: Dr. Loosens' amazingly floral Wehlenher Sonnenuhr Riesling Kabinett 2005 (German white wine)

2. Spectacular

Spectacular

I love parties and I love making dinner, but I hate the phrase "dinner party." It makes me think of formality, napkin rings, and good behavior, none of which I want around the house when my friends come over to eat. I like my big meals to be noisy, messy, spectacular, and raucous—celebrations rather than appreciations.

So the dishes in this chapter aren't just meals—they are spectacles that are more than the sum of their parts, and they will, inevitably, turn dinner into a party. Sure, they provide everything that a meal should: calories, protein, carbohydrates, fats, and fiber for you to metabolize into love and life. But they all have an extra extraordinary element to them that makes them fantastic. My favorites (and my favorite way of eating) are the interactive meals when your friends play an integral role in the cooking process, as with the marvelous Shabu-Shabu, Fondue Bourguignonne, and Cha Ca La Vong Noodles. There are other dishes that didn't quite make it into my top 101 but which are also fantastic interactive affairs, such as Japanese nabes, sukiyaki, and teppanyaki and Korean soondaes.

However, let's be honest. These aren't quick midweek suppers or TV dinners. Although many of the dishes in this chapter are cheap and easy to prepare, they are really Friday night or weekend meals. They are for special friends and family or for special occasions, often simply because they take a little more thought or planning, an extra piece of equipment, ingredients that you wouldn't necessarily have in your refrigerator if you hadn't planned ahead, or they simply require a cooking technique that you don't often deploy on the home cooking front.

But please don't be afraid of these dishes. Despite the fact that some of them seem daunting, they are all simple and practical dishes that may take a little more time than the average meal to prepare, but that's usually because you're making it for a crowd! I recently made the Grand Aoïli for 24 people at my daughter's christening, and it took me a while to prepare because of the sheer amount of food I was preparing, although the cooking of it was embarrassingly easy.

If you have some cash to spend and something big to celebrate, I thoroughly recommend the Suckling Pig. It's not cheap, but you and your friends will never forget eating it, so it doesn't feel so bad to splash out on it as long as you don't do it every week. If you're on a budget or you have kids, I thoroughly recommend the Polenta alla Spianatora, which everyone goes wild about because it feels so naughty!

These are outrageously fun dishes to make and to eat. When your best friends are coming around and you want to show them how much you love them, or if you have unfamiliar friends mixing for the first time, these are the dishes you need. They break down barriers and turn eating into exhilaration; they create an atmosphere of fun and interaction that makes any dinner into a party. Not a dinner party, you understand— just dinner that also happens to be a party.

⑪ Suckling pig

This is probably the most spectacular, sumptuous, and outrageously decadent dish I've ever cooked. It's the definitive feast and, although it's surprisingly easy to make, it's definitely not for the fainthearted. Serving an entire pig is a bold, loud, and graphic statement that shouts "I AM A CARNIVORE" very loudly indeed.

Suckling pigs are justifiably expensive. The animals are slaughtered at anything from two to eight weeks old and they have, as their names suggest, been raised only on their mothers' milk. Hence, the meat (especially the belly, where the spareribs and bacon come from) is extraordinarily sweet and tender, and the cracklings are out of this world.

The easiest way to cook this is oven-roasted, although you can also spit-roast it over a fire or grill if you have the time and the tools. During cooking, it's best to place a stone in the pig's mouth to keep it open, and then to replace that with an apple when it's nearly finished. Also, I highly recommend that you bring the entire pig to the table for carving so that everyone gets the full spectacle and offers the little guy the full respect to which he's due.

How big is your oven?

Measure your oven before ordering your pig. A 35-inch/90-cm oven will easily fit most suckling pigs, but if it's narrower, you may need to have the pig cut in half.

Tongan feeding frenzy

You wouldn't want to be a pig on Tonga around church conference season, when worshipers get together for a no-holds-barred week of round-the-clock feasting. I tagged along with one church and helped out with the cooking. They had 12 suckling pigs on spits over a large open fire for each meal, while members of the congregation had cooked several each at home as well. All the members of the church got together under one roof with their food, and there was so much that the tables were double-decked, with shelves running down the middle carrying back-to-back suckling pigs. There were three main feasts each day, although I could only manage two.

ingredients

Serves 8–10

13 lb/6 kg suckling pig, intestines removed and ready to cook

extra virgin olive oil

16 garlic cloves

handful of thyme sprigs

8 bay leaves

1 small apple

generous $^1/_3$ cup white wine, Marsala, or dessert wine

salt and pepper

Roast Potatoes (see page 113), garlic, and vegetables, and applesauce, to serve

To drink: A good spicy South African Pinotage (red wine)

method

Preheat the oven to 375°F/190°C. Wash the pig thoroughly and pat dry. Rub oil and salt and pepper all over it, then wrap little pieces of foil around the ears and tail and secure with a toothpick. Place a rock (not an apple) between the pig's teeth.

Lay the garlic, thyme, and bay leaves in the bottom of a large roasting pan. Place the pig on top and put in the oven. After 30 minutes, baste the pig with more oil and reduce the oven temperature to 350°F/180°C. Cook for an additional $1^3/_4$ hours, basting every 20 minutes. If you are serving vegetables, start roasting them after 2 hours. Heat the broiler to high, and place the pig under it to turn the fat crispy (making sure that it doesn't burn). Remove the pig and replace the stone with an apple. Lift off the cracklings and set aside, then wrap the pig in foil and let rest for up to 1 hour.

Pour any excess fat out of the pan, then add the wine and place over medium heat to reduce by half, stirring in any nice crusty sediment to make the gravy.

Carve at the table to loud applause and serve with the cracklings, roast potatoes, garlic, and vegetables, and some applesauce.

⑫ Soft-shelled crabs in tempura batter

Question: When can you eat an entire crab—shell and all?

Answer: When it's a soft-shelled crab.

If you haven't seen one before, the idea of eating soft-shelled crab can be difficult to get your head around. Yes, you really do eat the entire crustacean: claws, head, legs, carapace. And, by some miracle of biology (see right), none of it is bony. In fact, it is delicate and sweet, with an interesting, but not off-putting set of soft-and-crunchy textures that work beautifully when the crab has been swiftly deep-fried in a light, crispy tempura batter.

Soft-shelled crabs can be difficult to buy fresh. But fear not, because there's a growing industry in cultivating and freezing these little guys. Your nearest fish dealer or Japanese, Chinese, or Thai supermarket will probably hide little boxes of these in their freezers. I thoroughly recommend transferring them to your own freezer at your earliest convenience. The crabs themselves are about 3–4 inches/7.5–10 cm wide and are often wrapped in little discardable plastic sleeves to keep them from molding together into a block of crabby ice.

This is one of those meals that you have to cook a portion at a time while everyone starts eating around you—if there's too much food in the deep fat fryer, the temperature will reduce and everything will become soggy and too fatty. But at least there'll be a round of applause as you sit down to eat your own.

What is a soft-shelled crab?

These really are little miracles of science. A crab's shell is solid and doesn't grow with the crustacean itself, so once a year, when the crab has outgrown its armor, it molts and sheds its old shell before growing a new one. The crab is nude, soft, and vulnerable for up to two months, pumped with water to simulate the new, larger size it plans to be, during which time it has to hide from predators and hence can't eat.

Shortcut

If you're a bit lazy, don't worry: store-bought tempura batter mix works absolutely fine, if you can find it in your nearest Asian supermarket. And while you're there, pick up a bottle of ponzu—an amazing sweet citrus and soy dipping sauce.

method

Drain the thawed crabs, then gently squeeze them to get rid of excess water, being careful not to damage them.

Just before you're ready to cook, beat the eggs in a large bowl, then add the water, flour, cornstarch, and a pinch of salt, stirring gently with a fork so that they mix together. Don't beat the batter—it should remain a little lumpy.

Heat the oil in a deep-fat fryer to 375°F/190°C, or until a cube of bread browns in 30 seconds. Dip the crabs into the batter and then deep-fry two at a time, for 2–4 minutes, until crispy. They should still be a little soft inside. Drain on paper towels and sprinkle with salt. Serve them straight away with sushi rice, then dip the vegetables into the batter and deep-fry them in batches for around 40 seconds. Drain them on paper towels, sprinkle with salt, and serve with soy sauce and ponzu, if using. Continue cooking until all the ingredients have been used up.

ingredients

Serves 6 as a main course (halve the quantities for an appetizer)

12 frozen soft-shelled crabs, thawed

2 eggs

1³/₄ cups very cold water

scant 1¹/₂ cups all-purpose flour

scant ³/₄ cup cornstarch

vegetable oil, for deep-frying

2 large heads broccoli, cut into small florets

2 zucchini, thinly sliced lengthwise

salt

To serve

cooked sushi rice

soy sauce

ponzu (optional)

To drink: Very cold French Viogner (white wine)

⑬ Salt-crust chicken

You might have seen this odd-sounding cooking method on a few restaurant menus. I've decided to make it my mission to get people making it more often at home, for two good reasons: it's a wonderful way of steam-baking chicken, guinea fowl, or fish, and it's a spectacular way to present food.

You may think that this way of cooking would produce very salty food, but the salt crust is only there to create a tight-fitting casing that helps to keep the flavor locked into the food. When you bring the entire salt-crust mound to the table, smash into it carefully and then lay it all aside. Inside the crust will be deliciously tender meat cooked in steam.

The camel salt train

This will be of no use to your cooking, but it's fascinating nonetheless. In the Danakil region of northern Ethiopia and Southern Eritrea lies an extraordinary salt mine. Salt is a rare commodity in this area, being so far from the sea, so men drive their camels 240 miles/400 km from Mekele town to the infernal heat of the Danakil Depression and back, picking up salt and taking it for sale in towns and villages. It must be one of the grimmest trips on the planet, and even the toughest Ethiopians themselves admire the fortitude and bravery of the men who drive the salt trains. On the way there, the camels carry straw that they drop off at villages to be picked up on the way back—nothing grows in the Danakil. Each camel carries up to 198 lb/90 kg of salt blocks, cut out of the huge, dead salt lake. The salt is so valuable back in town that it's known as white gold.

method

Preheat the oven to 425°F/220°C. Wipe and untruss the chicken. Line a roasting pan with foil, overlapping it so that it will wrap around the chicken.

In a large bowl, mix all the other ingredients, except the garlic, together. Lay one third of the mixture in the roasting pan, making an indentation in the middle. Place the garlic cloves in the indentation. Firmly press the bird breast-side down on top of them, then use the rest of the salt mixture to cover it. It should be fully encased. If not, use more salt.

Place the roasting pan in the oven and bake for 1 hour. Remove the chicken from the oven, then let stand for 25 minutes.

Take the chicken to the table, break open the crust, taking in a huge lungful of the aromas that are released, then discard it. Beware of clumsiness: This is the point at which salt can get mixed in with the meat.

Serve with sautéed potatoes and zucchini salad.

ingredients

Serves 4 as a main course

1 x 3 lb 5 oz /1.5 kg chicken
4 lb 8 oz/2 kg rock salt
zest of 2 lemons
2 large handfuls chopped thyme
2 large handfuls chopped rosemary
2 tbsp water
10 garlic cloves, unpeeled
sautéed potatoes and a salad of thinly-sliced
zucchini mixed with lemon and olive oil,
to serve

To drink: Chilean or New Zealand Merlot or Cabernet Sauvignon

⑭ Pig's feet

The first time I ate pig's feet was in Barcelona, Spain, and it was very nearly disastrous. I had taken my girlfriend for a surprise romantic weekend break, and it was going really, really badly. She knew that I was going to take her away somewhere, but for some reason I had led her to think it would be a cycling vacation somewhere cold and windy. When I drove off the highway toward the airport she started to panic, and when I checked us in to a flight to Barcelona she looked bereft. What could possibly be wrong with a romantic break to one of the most glamorous cities on the planet? "Because I've packed sweaters and sneakers, you fool," she said. I realized, not for the first time, that I really don't understand women.

We checked into a hotel that had looked really good in the pictures, but which had clearly spent more on its photographer than its decorator. We went for long walks hand-in-hand along beaches and Las Ramblas, me trying to put a brave face on it with a forced grin, and my girlfriend perspiring heavily under a thick layer of wool.

We wandered into a restaurant on the seafront and I ordered the pig's feet. The Spanish know a thing or two about dealing with pigs, and I had always seen feet in stores but had never tried them. Here was my chance.

The plate of feet that was put in front of me was a triumph of pig over appetite. It looked like a bomb had gone off at the butcher. I picked through the parts on the plate: bone, skin, and sinew but no meat. I thought that they

were playing a joke on me, the funny, irascible foreigner. I called the waiter over to receive the full force of my wrath, but he kindly and patiently explained that pig's feet never have any meat—you're supposed to pick through the bones and eat the gelatinous, silken skin and sinew. My girlfriend and I laughed for the first time on the vacation, and, as we laughed, the tension between us crumbled, making us laugh all the harder until we were breathless. When we had recovered, we tried the feet again, and were transported by the deep, gelatinous flavors and textures and we understood. It was a turning point both for our vacation and for our palates.

I know that most people see pig's feet as bizarre and possibly even distasteful, but I recommend that you take a deep breath and try them because they are delicious. And if you serve them to your friends you'll probably be pleasantly surprised at how many people try them, rather than how few.

There are two distinct approaches to cooking feet. You can go the whole hog and cook them from scratch for hours on end, gently and skillfully coaxing them into an edible dish. Or you can do what every sensible French cook does and buy them already cooked from the butchers so that they just need to be broiled.

How to deal with feet

Let's assume that you have taken the rational
option and found precooked feet at the
butcher's. If they haven't already been sliced
lengthwise in two, ask the butcher to do this for
you. Heat the broiler to medium
and lay the feet in a heatproof
dish, cut-side up. Cover them
with a mixture of bread crumbs,
crushed garlic, butter, chopped
parsley, and salt and pepper and
then place them under the broiler, not
too close to the heat. Broil gently for
15–20 minutes, making sure that they
become crisp on the top but don't burn.
You're just trying to heat them up, really.
Serve with mustard, bread, and a bowl for
the bones. Only about 50 percent of the
trotter is really edible; the rest is bone. But
don't let that worry you.

**To drink:
A good red Rioja**

⑮ Lamb roasted in a lemon and thyme crust

Whenever I ponder my desert island dishes (this happens pretty much daily), I start with the exotic ones and the memorable life-defining dishes, but eventually I'll come around to one of my familiar, simple favorites: roast lamb. This version is the most spectacular of all roast lamb dishes.

The idea is to cover the lamb in a fragrant casing of whole, finely chopped lemons (this is easily taken care of with a food processor) combined with garlic, salt, and herbs. It is breathtakingly good, encasing the lamb and suffusing it with a deep citrus flavor, helping it to cook evenly and gently.

The gravy is deliciously citrus-flavored, too, but beware; after cooking, you need to remove and discard most of the lemon crust, and add it to the gravy bit by bit—the lemon can make the gravy a little bitter if you're not careful.

Variation

Stop right there! If it's blood orange season, you should substitute those for the lemons—it'll be mind-blowingly good.

The fat-tailed sheep

I had seen line drawings of fat-tailed sheep in food history books, but I didn't really believe that they existed until I visited Afghanistan and met them. They don't really have that fat a tail, but rather a huge wobbly hump of fat that sits on their bottom above the tail. I was interested to discover that the fat is as valuable, if not more valuable, than the meat itself. It's light and fluffy—not like traditional lamb fat—and an essential ingredient for making lamb kebabs, which usually consist of one piece of fat to each piece of meat. It's also used to make Quabili rice—basically a dish of rice, a few vegetables, and a lot of stewed lamb, all oozing lamb fat.

ingredients

Serves 6 as a main course

5 lb 8 oz–6 lb 8 oz/2.5–3 kg leg of lamb
generous 1 cup chicken stock
generous 1 cup red wine
1 tbsp red currant sauce

Marinade

1 bulb of garlic, cloves separated but unpeeled
5 lemons or blood oranges
1 tbsp fresh rosemary leaves, chopped
1 tbsp fresh thyme leaves
2 tbsp salt

To serve

Roast Potatoes (see page 113)
glazed carrots
mint sauce

method

Remove the lamb from the refrigerator and pat dry with paper towels. Combine all the marinade ingredients in a food processor and blend to a paste. Place the lamb in a roasting pan and cover with the paste so that it is completely encased. Cover loosely with foil and set aside in a cool place for an hour (or preferably in your refrigerator overnight).

If the lamb has been in the refrigerator, remove it 30 minutes before cooking. Preheat the oven to 400°F/200°C. Put the foil-covered lamb into the oven and cook for $1^3/4$ hours. Take it out of the roasting pan, reserve 2 tablespoons of the marinade paste, and let the lamb rest in the foil for 15–20 minutes.

Meanwhile, put the roasting pan on the stove and simmer the marinade paste with the stock, wine, and red currant sauce until reduced by about half.

Carve the lamb, discarding most of the paste, and serve with the gravy, roast potatoes, carrots, and mint sauce.

To drink: A good Pinot Noir from Burgundy (red wine)

(16) Shabu-shabu

Equipment

You do need a specific piece of equipment for making this, but it's one that most people will have if they've ever been camping: a little gas burner or a fondue pot with burner. Some of those very cheap wooden disposable chopsticks would be good, too.

This is a very cool Japanese version of the famous Chinese steamboat or Mongolian hotchpotch, where a selection of raw meats and vegetables is laid out on the table around a central pot of simmering broth, and the diners cook their meal for themselves by dipping the food into it. The Japanese think that the noise of the meat being waved through the liquid sounds like "shabu-shabu" (which just goes to prove that one man's onomatopoeia is another man's gobbledygook).

This interactive style of feasting is my favorite way to eat, because it's fun and rowdy, and everybody really gets to grips with their food. It's also remarkably good for you because it's low in fat and super-fresh. It's the fondue for the twenty-first century!

Shabu-shabu is a fantastic way to get your guests relaxed and having fun with each other, and it's especially good for breaking the ice for a group who don't know each other very well. The cooking process becomes a communal affair and a team effort as people steal each other's food, help each other cook, and swap tips on sauce combinations. A word of warning: It's not a great dish for young kids because of that saucepan of simmering water.

How to eat shabu-shabu

Pick up whichever meat and vegetables you like, using chopsticks (or slotted spoons), and dip briefly in the stock to cook. The best beef really shouldn't take more than a few seconds—you don't want it boiled—just blanched.

When everyone's had their fill of meat, drop in some noodles, then serve in bowls as a broth to cleanse the palate.

ingredients

Serves 6 as a main course

4 lemongrass stalks, bashed with a rolling pin
large handful of fresh cilantro, roots and leaves
1 large red chile, halved lengthwise
1-inch/2.5-cm piece fresh ginger, thickly sliced
2 lb 4 oz/1 kg large cooked shell-on shrimp, shells and heads removed and reserved
10 cups water
3 chicken breasts, skinned and very thinly sliced
1 whole pork tenderloin, very thinly sliced across the grain
500 g/1 lb 2 oz beef tenderloin, sliced as thinly as possible
1 bundle enoki mushrooms
1/2 Chinese cabbage, leaves separated and halved
1 large head broccoli, broken up into small florets
4 carrots, cut diagonally into thin slices

Sauce

generous 1/4 cup soy sauce
3 1/2 tbsp mirin
3 1/2 tbsp rice vinegar
2 scallions, finely chopped
2 tsp grated fresh ginger
1 egg yolk

To serve

cooked egg noodles
ponzu
soy sauce

method

Put the lemongrass, cilantro, chile, ginger, reserved shrimp shells, and water into a large saucepan and simmer over low heat for about 1 hour. Remove from the heat, strain into a fondue pot, and discard the solids.

Lay out the meat and the shrimp on serving plates and put in the refrigerator. Lay the vegetables on serving plates. Make the sauce by combining all the ingredients and mixing with a fork. Divide between three small bowls.

Place a tabletop burner in the middle of the table, and put the fondue pot on it over low heat so that it simmers gently. Place the plates of meat and vegetables and sauces around the table. Serve some ponzu and soy sauce in bowls on the side.

Give everyone soup bowls and chopsticks and encourage them to start cooking their own food—meat and shrimp first, then vegetables. Each piece of food will take 10–60 seconds to cook, and it should then be fished out, dipped in one of the sauces, and eaten.

When all the main ingredients are finished, add the cooked noodles, then ladle them out with the broth for a nice, clean, head-clearing soup.

To drink:
Japanese beer,
followed by
some good sake

⑰ Polenta alla spianatora
(Cornmeal served on the table)

This recipe is an outrage to modern table manners, a regression to an age before tableware, and a shocking mess. All of which makes it liberating, sexy, and loads of fun. There's an extraordinary frisson of excitement and disbelief among your guests when you spread the cornmeal straight onto the table, then drop your ragù into the middle and hand the forks around.

Of course, if your guests think that it's all a little déclassé, you can inform them that this ancient serving method is common in many regions of Italy, where the locals think that eating from plates is for wimps. You can even buy a spianatora—a large wooden board that sits on the table.

If you're cooking for kids, you won't need to make excuses; they'll be beside themselves with excitement and the sheer naughtiness of it all!

What is polenta?

The word "polenta" has its roots in the Latin "pulmentum," and was originally made from barley, spelt, chickpea, or even walnut flour—maize didn't arrive in Italy until about 1650 as part of the great Columbian Exchange, whereby foods, culture, and people crossed between the eastern and western hemispheres. Before then, there were no potatoes, tomatoes, or chocolate in Europe, and no oranges, cattle, or wheat in the Americas. Nowadays, the word "polenta" is used to refer to cornmeal.

ingredients

Serves 8 as a main course

4 tbsp olive oil

2 lb/900 g sausage meat, or Italian sausages, meat removed from the casings

2 large onions, finely chopped

2 large fennel bulbs, or 14 oz/400 g celery

6 garlic cloves, peeled and chopped

generous $^1/_4$ cup red wine

1 lb 12 oz/800 g canned chopped plum tomatoes

1 tsp sugar

large handful of fresh basil, roughly torn

3 liters water

1 lb 2 oz/500 g cornmeal

1 $^3/_4$ cups freshly grated Parmesan cheese, plus extra to serve

salt and pepper

method

Put a wide, heavy-bottom saucepan or casserole over medium–high heat and add 1 tablespoon of olive oil. Add the sausage meat, spread it out across the bottom of the pan, and fry it without stirring for about 15 minutes, until it begins to brown on one side. Break it up with a wooden spoon, remove from the pan, and set aside. Pour off any excess fat.

Reduce the heat to low, add the rest of the olive oil, the onions, and fennel and fry gently for 15–20 minutes, until softened, then add the garlic and fry for an additional 5 minutes. Increase the heat to medium, add the wine, and let it bubble for a minute, then add the tomatoes, sugar, and cooked sausage meat, reduce the heat, and simmer gently for an additional 20 minutes. Check the seasoning and mix in the basil, reserving some to garnish. All of this can be done the day before.

Bring the water almost to a boil with 1 tablespoon of salt and add the cornmeal. Simmer gently for about 30 minutes, until it has a creamy mashed potato consistency. Add most of the grated cheese and stir it in.

Clean the table. Spread the cornmeal on the table in two bowl-shaped portions, so that everyone can reach it, and spoon the ragù into the middle. Garnish with basil, sprinkle a little cheese over the top, and tuck in.

To drink: A good Chianti

(18) Fondue Bourguignonne

I'm not sure why I should feel so embarrassed to make this admission, but I love fondues. It's true that they are synonymous with the 1970s, polyester flares, and sideburns, but there's nothing bad about that in my book (although I do draw the line at dropping keys into bowls). Perhaps the collaborative touchy-feely nature of fondue makes some people feel a little tense, but in these days of interactive experiences this kind of dish is making a comeback, and not a moment too soon.

Bourguignonne is a wonderful version of this and it couldn't be more different from the cheesy mess that has become associated with the word "fondue." Instead, a pot of hot oil sits in the middle of the table and everyone gathers around dipping cubes of beef in it to sear them before eating.

Let's think practically about this: You can't make this dish unless you have a fondue pot, a tabletop burner, or a sturdy camping stove. You can't just put the pot on the stove and transfer it to the table because the oil will quickly cool so that it won't sear the meat. Incidentally, because of the hot oil on the table, this isn't the best dish to serve when you have small children eating with you.

What went wrong with fondue?

I think the decline of the fondue is more to do with the dreadful schnapps-laden cheese fondues that so many people were served in bad Alpine restaurants while on skiing trips. I was put off them for years by one served in the French Alps that had been made with cheap cheese and far too much rough hooch. There's no point beating about the bush—badly-made cheese fondue tastes disGUSting!

ingredients

Serves 6 as a main course

2 lb 4 oz/1 kg sirloin steak
4 cups sunflower oil

Garlic butter
1 garlic clove, crushed
$^3/_4$ cup butter, softened

Salsa verde
$4^1/_2$ tbsp olive oil
large handful of fresh parsley,
roughly chopped
large handful of fresh basil
2 tbsp capers, drained and rinsed
2 tbsp chopped pickled gherkins
1 garlic clove, crushed
4 anchovy fillets
squeeze of lemon juice
1 tsp mustard

To serve
Béarnaise Sauce (see page 105)
Garlic Butter
Salsa Verde
French fries
crisp salad

method

To make the garlic butter, beat the garlic into the butter and let stand at room temperature for about 1 hour. Make the salsa verde by placing all of the ingredients in a food processor and pulsing until you have a nice lumpy sauce.

Trim any fat or sinew from the meat, then cut it into bite-size cubes and divide evenly between two plates.

Divide the sauces between several bowls and distribute them around the table. Place a tabletop gas burner in the middle of the table and put a heavy-bottom saucepan on top (or use a fondue set, if you have one). Add the sunflower oil and heat to 375°F/190°C, or until a cube of bread turns brown within 30 seconds. Put the French fries and salad on the table so that everyone can tuck in.

Using long metal or wooden kebab sticks, each person skewers a cube of meat and then carefully places it in the hot oil to cook to their preference. They then transfer the meat to their plates and let it cool briefly before dipping in sauce and eating.

To drink: A really hefty European Georgian red, if you can find some

⑲ Cha ca la vong sweet-sour noodle soup with nuoc nam

This sparkling fish and noodle soup has that extra edge because it's fun and interactive, assembled individually by each person from a range of ingredients at the table. The difference here is that it's based on a set of flavors that just somehow fit together seamlessly, like so many sweet-sour, fish-sauce-based Southeast Asian dishes.

The dish originated at a Vietnamese restaurant called Cha Ca La Vong, which has branches in Hanoi and Saigon, but it's so good that it has entered legend and been adapted and updated so that anyone can make it with ingredients found in most supermarkets.

The trick with Cha Ca La Vong noodles is to encourage everyone to experiment, and not to create one big meal in a bowl, but to make little bowls each time so that they can play with flavor combinations over two or three attempts. Trouble is, it tastes so good that this is pretty much impossible.

Vietnamese and Thai ingredients

The recipe below is adapted for people who don't have access to a Vietnamese, Thai, or Chinese supermarket, but if you do, try using pungent Thai basil instead of normal basil, galangal instead of ginger, and catfish (which you can usually get frozen).

To drink: A crisp, light, gooseberryish Sauvignon blanc white wine

ingredients

Serves 6

4 garlic cloves, crushed

1-inch/2.5-cm piece fresh ginger,
peeled and grated

2 tsp ground turmeric

1 tbsp fish sauce

$^1/_2$ tbsp sugar

$^1/_2$ red chile, chopped

1 lb 10 oz/750 g whitefish fillets,
cut into small chunks

4 tbsp sunflower oil

2 tbsp water

2 large bunches dill, chopped (stalks included)

Nuoc nam

2 garlic cloves, crushed

$^1/_2$ red chile, sliced

3 tbsp superfine sugar

juice of 2 limes

4 tbsp fish sauce

1 tbsp rice vinegar

1 tbsp water

To serve

1 lb 2 oz/500 g rice noodles, cooked

14 oz/400 g baby spinach

1 bunch scallions, chopped

2 large bunches fresh basil

$1^3/_4$ cups roasted peanuts, roughly chopped

method

Mix the garlic, ginger, turmeric, fish sauce, sugar, and chile together, then add the fish. Mix gently so that all the fish chunks are well-coated in the spice paste and let marinate, preferably overnight (although 1 hour would be sufficient).

Make the nuoc nam by combining the ingredients in a bowl and stirring until the sugar dissolves.

When you're ready to eat, heat the oil in a wok or heavy-bottom skillet until very hot, then fry the chunks of fish in it for $1^1/_2$ minutes on each side. Turn off the heat and add the water (be careful—it may spit) and the dill. Cover so that the dill wilts in the steam.

Place the fish in bowls on the table (if you have a tabletop burner or hotplate, put this on the table and place the fish on it to keep warm). Put the noodles, spinach, scallions, basil, and peanuts in separate bowls and serve on the side. Each person should take a bowl, place some noodles in the bottom, then add any combination of ingredients that they like.

㉒ Grand aïoli

I fell in love with this legendary dish of vegetables, poached fish, and garlicky mayonnaise when I saw a photo of it in a fabulously glamorous hotel in the south of France, served accompanied by whole cauliflowers and heads of broccoli. It just looked so cool and cheeky to serve food that casually! It was only later that I realized that all the vegetables had been carefully blanched, and their presentation was a fine and complex balance, but by then my desire had been aroused.

The perfect grand aïoli should *look* as if it's been casually thrown together by a lazy cook who really only bothered to go shopping. It's only when people start digging into it that they realize the art and love that has gone into it.

The confidence of the serving method is all important. You should place all the ingredients in the middle of the table so that everyone can reach, and then sit back and enjoy yourself, leading the way by tucking in with abandon, and then watching everyone follow. They will be a little nonplussed at first, but will soon get the hang of it.

Needless to say, this is a wonderful dish to eat in the summer (although I confess that I love it so much I serve it at all times of the year). The ingredients involved are all relatively basic, and the serving method even more so, so it's all the more important to make sure that you buy the best that's available.

Straying from the path of fishy righteousness

Purists will faint at the thought, but I like using a large slab of salmon for this. It's unusual, because it's traditionally made using cod or haddock, but with stocks of these fish running perilously low in many places, I think that it's time to look around. And there are few fishy delights that can beat a lightly poached piece of wild salmon married with aïoli.

ingredients

Serves 8 as a rich main course

1 lb 2 oz/500 g new potatoes
14 oz/400 g green beans, trimmed
1 lb 2 oz/500 g small or baby carrots, halved
lengthwise
1 lb 2 oz/500 g baby zucchini, halved lengthwise
1 large cauliflower, cut into florets
1 large head broccoli, cut into florets
1 lb 2 oz/500 g tomatoes, quartered
crusty bread, to serve

Court bouillon

8 cups water
scant 1 cup white wine
1 carrot, finely sliced
1 celery stalk, finely sliced
1/2 onion, finely sliced
1/2 tsp black peppercorns
2 tsp salt
1 bay leaf

3 lb 5 oz/1.5 kg fillet of salmon or cod, skinned and
pin boned

Aïoli

4 fat garlic cloves, roughly chopped
2 egg yolks
1 tsp Dijon mustard
scant 1 cup extra virgin olive oil
1 1/4 cups sunflower oil
1 tbsp lemon juice
4 tbsp cold water
salt and pepper

method

Place all the court bouillon ingredients in a large roasting pan or fish kettle. Simmer for 15 minutes, then add the fish and, when it returns to a simmer, reduce the heat to as low as possible so the liquid just shudders occasionally. Poach, covered, for 5 minutes, then set aside to cool, covered.

To make the aïoli, combine the garlic, egg yolks, and mustard in a food processor. Pulse, slowly pouring in the oils one after the other in a slow, regular trickle—they will eventually thicken into a firm, thick, fluffy mayonnaise. Add the lemon juice and cold water, season generously, and give it one extra zap. Divide evenly between two or three bowls.

Bring a large saucepan of lightly salted water to a boil, add the potatoes, and cook for 10–15 minutes, until just tender. Bring separate saucepans of water to a boil and steam the remaining vegetables, except the tomatoes, for 2–4 minutes each. They should be lightly blanched and retain a good crunch. Put the fish in the middle of a large platter, if you have one (or on several plates if you don't), and surround it with all the vegetables and the aïoli. Give everyone a plate, then encourage them to put some aïoli on it and help themselves to vegetables for dipping.

To drink: A very cold white Burgundy

3. Expensive

Expensive

You don't have to spend a lot of money to eat wonderful food. However...

I'm not a regular habitué of fancy restaurants, but every now and then I allow myself guilty pleasures by saving up my pocket money in order to avail myself of the finest ingredients on the earth. And I must say, I love those moments. Sometimes we need to celebrate events, and sometimes we just need to remind ourselves of the joys of treating ourselves to an insane flight of fancy.

Yesterday I stopped off at my favorite Spanish deli, and the moment I spied the Pata Negra ham, I knew that I was a lost cause. That stuff has a strange and indomitable magnetic power over me. I see it sitting there smugly on the counter, draped in its shroud of sculpted shards of fat to keep its precious flesh from drying out, and it winks at me with a come-hither look. Once it's hooked me into its orbit I know that I am lost. So, I came home with a small wrapped parcel of the tiniest slivers of the precious ham and guiltily showed my wife. She did the decent thing: she frowned at me for my profligacy, ruffled my hair as if I were a naughty toddler, then reached for the Manzanilla sherry. We sat on the kitchen table munching and offering thanks until it was gone. Pure happiness.

What's interesting is that some of the foods in this chapter may be expensive now, but they used to be held in pretty low regard. Oysters used to be a poor man's food, added to pies to make up bulk. Porcini and truffles may be expensive at the market, but at source they are free foods that grow in the wild, and are generally foraged for by one man and his dog (or pig). On the other hand, I readily admit that toro tuna and kobe beef are just plain outrageously expensive, but they are also outrageously good—carefully and lovingly hunted or reared to deliver to us the most refined tastes imaginable.

The one odd ingredient in this chapter is gold. I know that it may sound strange and even a little distasteful to cook with something that is purely about spectacle and nothing to do with taste or flavor, but I also believe that if you can make a meal that is so memorable that you and your friends will remember a single mouthful of gilded food for the rest of your lives, you will be a better person for it. When you take stock of the most extraordinary things you did and some of the adventures you went on, some of them should be about food. Is it better to wear gold around your neck than to eat it? Not as far as I'm concerned.

The most important thing to remember is that all of the dishes and ingredients here may be rare and wonderful, but familiarity breeds contempt. These are foods for special occasions, and if you had loads of cash to throw at food (oh, if only), you'd be in danger of growing bored with it. Eat as wide a range of foods as you can.

The most expensive foods don't necessarily provide us with the best textures and flavors. I ate smileys (slow-cooked sheep's heads) a week ago in a South African township and the eyeball was the softest, most unctuous sliver of meat I've ever put in my mouth. Chefs across the world do unmentionable things to ducks to achieve a texture like that, yet in Mzoli's meat shack, that texture was available for just $2. It may sound dreadful to you, but it proves that sometimes the cheap stuff can be the best.

Enjoy these outrageously expensive foods, but don't get stuck on them. Dabble, and keep them for special occasions, and they will always deliver a little slice of magic.

㉑ White truffle risotto

I was once an impoverished young waiter. I loved my job because it allowed me proximity to the finest ingredients on the planet, but at the same time I was wildly jealous of the customers who toyed nonchalantly with their food. The most upsetting moment was seeing a lovingly made truffle risotto being returned almost untouched. I sat mourning it and inhaling the deep, musky, truffley smell for ages before finally dropping it into the trash.

The next day I called in sick and went searching for the finest truffle in town. Tragically for my bank balance, I found it, and, after assembling a week's wages, I purchased it. It was about the size of my thumb, and I fell head over heels in love with it. I sat it in a bed of arborio rice in a small jar, and opened it every now and then for a sniff. I planned what I would do with it and I drew up a list of friends I should eat it with, who would appreciate it.

It was three weeks before I came to terms with saying good-bye to it. I invited ten friends over for a risotto, cooked the rice with love, and finally opened my jar. AAAAAAArgh! It was covered in mold! Disaster. I scraped the mold off and persevered, grating it over the velvety rice in the hope that all was not lost. It was. Too little, too old.

The best ways to eat truffles are the simplest: Grated on scrambled eggs, mashed potato, or risotto. But be warned: They don't necessarily go a long way. Get as much truffle as you can afford and share it with as few of your closest friends as your conscience allows.

Truffle

Truffles are underground fungi, often black in the Perigord, France, and white in Alba in Italy, and are usually hunted using dogs or pigs from late October to February. My daughter Poppy says the smell is "yuk," my daughter Daisy says it's "yummy." It's my favorite smell in the world.

I bought a truffle tree once—an oak sapling with roots impregnated with truffle spores—and it cost a king's ransom. It was dead from overwatering within two months. Which just proves the saying that "too much love can kill you."

ingredients

Serves 4 as a main course

small handful of dried porcini
generous $^1/_2$ cup unsalted butter
1 small onion, finely chopped
1 fennel bulb, or a small head of celery,
finely chopped
1 garlic clove, finely chopped
$1^1/_2$ cups risotto rice
4 cups warm chicken stock
4 tbsp Vermouth
generous $^1/_3$ cup heavy cream
$1^1/_4$ cups finely grated Parmesan cheese
1–2 oz/25–55 g white truffles (or as much
as you can afford), cleaned

method

Place the porcini in a cup and cover them with warm water. Let rehydrate for at least 10 minutes.

Melt three quarters of the butter in a wide, heavy-bottom saucepan and slowly fry the onion and fennel, stirring frequently, until softened and translucent. Add the garlic and rice and fry for 2 minutes, stirring frequently.

Add the porcini and the porcini-flavored water and then start adding the warm stock a ladleful at a time, stirring so that the rice doesn't stick, and letting it absorb the stock before adding the next ladleful. Continue until the rice grains are soft on the outside but with a slight firmness in the middle (you may not need to use all the liquid).

Add the Vermouth, cream, half the Parmesan cheese, and the remaining butter and stir through.

Serve on warmed plates, sprinkle with the remaining Parmesan cheese, then shave some truffle over each portion using a vegetable peeler.

To drink: A spicy Pinotage or a fruity Pinot Noir red wine

㉒ Lobster salad with herbed mayonnaise à la Parisienne

The tender, succulent meat from a lobster has such a delicate flavor that it's best to do little more than poach it and garnish it with delicate herbs and a light mayonnaise. I really don't understand the fascination with lobster thermidor—the idea of coating such refined meat in cheese seems so wrong. Keep it clean and serene!

Lobster is, justifiably, another highly expensive ingredient, and should be reserved for special occasions, but you don't need to go overboard; although these ancient creatures contain a relatively small amount of flesh, it's beguilingly rich and extraordinarily filling.

Le Repertoire de la Cuisine

This extraordinary book has no place on your bookshelf unless you, like me, enjoy wasting hours reading about weird, ancient, and largely irrelevant food arcana. It's a sort of Escoffier offshoot, explaining the infuriating naming system of French cuisine so that you can work out the difference between Homard Chantecler (curried lobster served with cockscombs) and Homard Cardinal (poached lobster with sauce Mornay). You can often trace the history of a dish through the name of its inventor, patron, or champion, should you so desire. Apart from that, it's wonderfully useless.

ingredients

Serves 4 as a main course

2 live lobsters, around 1 lb 12 oz/750 g, or
1 lb 2 oz/500 g cooked fresh lobster meat

1 large cucumber

1 lettuce

4 hard-boiled eggs, halved

salt and pepper

steamed or boiled new potatoes and salad
leaves, to serve

Mayonnaise

2 egg yolks

1 tsp Dijon mustard

generous $^1/_3$ cup extra virgin olive oil

$^2/_3$ cup sunflower oil

1 tbsp lemon juice

4 tbsp cold water

small handful of parsley, finely chopped

small handful of dill, finely chopped

small handful of chervil leaves (optional),
finely chopped

salt and pepper

method

If using fresh lobsters put them into the freezer for
2 hours to kill them. Bring a large saucepan of heavily
salted water to a boil and add the lobsters. Return to a
boil and cook for 15 minutes. Remove from the heat,
drain, and let cool.

To make the mayonnaise, combine the egg yolks and
mustard in a food processor. Turn the processor on
and, with the motor running, pour in the olive oil
and then the sunflower oil in a slow, regular trickle,
until the mixture has a good thick consistency. Add
the lemon juice, water, and salt and pepper to taste
and pulse again. Fold the herbs through, then place in
a bowl and refrigerate.

Peel, halve, and seed the cucumber. Cut into thin
slivers using a vegetable peeler.

Cut the lobster in half lengthwise, remove the dark
vein that runs along the back of the tail, then remove
the stomach sac that sits behind the mouth. Crack the
claws with the back of a heavy knife.

Lay a bed of lettuce on each plate, scatter some
cucumber over, then lay two egg halves and the
halved lobsters on top. Season with salt and pepper,
add some herby mayonnaise, and serve with potatoes
and salad leaves.

To drink: A dry, floral Chilean
Gewürztraminer

㉓ Roast goose with old English apple stuffing

Goose is an iconic, ancient, and almost regal food inextricably associated with luxury and Christmas. It makes a rare and spectacular Christmas feast, but it's expensive because geese grow slowly, producing few eggs that take a long time—about a month—to hatch. But when you buy a goose, your money has been well spent because the meat is sweet and rich, and the fat that drains from the bird while you roast it is one of the greatest ingredients on the planet, never better than when used to make the greatest roast potatoes in the world.

Geese crop up throughout history and literature. The Romans adored them, and the French soon discovered a love for them. My favorite mention of goose is from Charles Dickens' *A Christmas Carol*, written at a time when it was a cheap and common substitute for the more expensive turkey (oh, if only that were still the case). Here, Scrooge watches Bob Cratchit's entire family enjoying one tiny goose:

"There never was such a goose. Bob said he didn't believe there ever was such a goose cooked. Its tenderness and flavor, size and cheapness, were the themes of universal admiration. Eked out by applesauce and mashed potatoes, it was a sufficient dinner for the whole family; indeed, as Mrs. Cratchit said with great delight (surveying one small atom of a bone upon the dish), they hadn't ate it all at last."

Foie gras—"fatty liver"

This is the enlarged liver of a goose or duck, made by force-feeding birds using a special funnel placed down their throats, a technique going back to classical Rome. But why do chefs love foie gras so much when it's so expensive and controversial? Well, it has an extraordinary texture and performance when cooked. Few substances remain so soft, while at the same time remaining solid. It is often added to other ingredients to make them smoother, creamier, and richer.

method

Remove the giblets from the bird and wipe it thoroughly inside with paper towels. Chop the liver and reserve for the stuffing.

Place a large saucepan over medium heat and add the butter. When the butter is melted add the onion, celery, and apples and slowly fry for about 20 minutes, until softened. Add the liver, carrots, bread crumbs, and sage and cook gently for an additional 15 minutes.

Preheat the oven to 425°F/220°C. Fill the main cavity of the bird with the stuffing and put any excess in an ovenproof bowl to cook alongside the goose. Rub the goose all over with salt and place it on a rack above a roasting pan. Roast for 30 minutes, then reduce the oven temperature to 350°F/180°C and continue to roast for an additional 1 1/2–2 hours (the bird is cooked when the juices run clear when the thigh is pricked with a skewer). Remove from the oven, cover, and let rest for 20 minutes.

Drain any excess fat from the pan (reserve and refrigerate it for making roast potatoes) and place the pan over medium heat. Add the wine and the stock, scraping up any crusty sediment from the bottom of the pan to make gravy. Simmer until reduced by half.

Scoop out the stuffing and carve the goose. Serve with roast potatoes and braised red cabbage.

ingredients

Serves 8 as a main course

10 lb/4.5 kg goose with giblets

5 tbsp butter

2 large onions, finely chopped

5 celery stalks, finely chopped

2 tart apples, peeled, cored, and chopped

2 carrots, grated

1 1/2 cups fresh bread crumbs

1 tbsp chopped fresh sage

generous 1/3 cup white wine

generous 1 cup chicken stock

salt

Roast Potatoes (see page 113) and Braised Red Cabbage (see page 130), to serve

To drink: A massive claret —a Bordeaux such as a grand cru St-Emilion

㉔ Toro tuna

Of all the memorable experiences in my life, only a handful of the really transcendental ones were purely sensory—all the others were partly psychological, fed by happiness, surprise, or love. Of the printable transcendental sensory experiences, most involve food, and my first mouthful of toro tuna—the revered fatty belly cut from a large fish—was one of those.

I first ate this served as two tiny lozenges of unassuming, pallid pink flesh. They would have seemed unpalatable and undramatic if they hadn't been served on a block of ice the size of a table, which gave a regal dignity to what otherwise could have been mistaken for processed meat. It was clear that this dish needed my full and undivided attention. I took my chopsticks and picked up a piece, watched all the time by a breathless waitress, and when I went to dip it in a little bowl of soy sauce, she motioned to me to just dip the tiniest corner. I put the tuna in my mouth.

I closed my eyes as I bit into the lozenge. Oh. My. God. It melted against my palate, releasing a flood of flavor throughout my mouth. I bit into it again and it seemed to swoon as it collapsed against my tongue. The flavor was delicate and strong at the same time, but it was the texture that blew me

away. When I opened my eyes, the waitress was still there, smiling gently. I nodded in thanks and she nodded back in understanding.

Some things should be cripplingly expensive, and toro tuna is one of those. I can afford to eat it only on very rare occasions, and that's a good thing. God forbid that one day I should find the sensation of eating something this extraordinary mundane. In fact, I hope I haven't ruined the experience for you by raising your expectations and telling you all about it. That would be a tragedy. Forget you ever read this!

To drink: A fine, clean water. You don't want anything messing with the flavors here

Tsukiji market

The tuna market in Tokyo is one of my favorite places in the world. If I could live there, I would. It's the world's biggest wholesale fish and seafood market, employing 60,000 workers, and it's full of strange and wonderful specimens of varying shapes and colors. But the market is really famous for its auctions of both fresh and frozen tuna. The fish lie on washed concrete floors in a series of vast warehouses and the buyers wander around with little picks, with which they test the flesh. They are looking for the fattiest, freshest fish. The auctions happen at a breathtaking pace, the buyers lurking on little banks of wooden steps, and the auctioneers shouting and gesticulating like bad actors. It's entirely incomprehensible to anyone who isn't a tuna trader, and it all happens in a flash. The public aren't allowed to buy at the auctions, and they aren't really supposed to buy from the middle men in the main market either, but if you ask nicely they might serve you. If they don't, it doesn't really matter because the market is also home to loads of fantastic sushi bars, where you can buy everything you've just seen, prepared by some of the finest fish ticklers on the planet. Go for the ones with the grubbiest door curtains—it's a sign that they are the most popular.

㉕ Kobe beef

Kobe beef is renowned for being the most expensive meat you can buy, and for good reason. The cows that it comes from are thought to be some of the most pampered livestock on the planet—they are massaged with sake and fed with beer and their owners supply music for them to listen to.

But why do they make such an effort? Simple: To create the most tender, soft, and fully flavored meat known to man. And does all the effort pay off? Ye gods, yes!

I first ate this in a spectacular restaurant at the top of a high-rise building overlooking Tokyo on a bright, clear day. The chef worked the tepanyaki grill like he was on center stage (which I suppose he was— we were filming him for a TV food show). These flat, stainless steel grills are the size of a large table, and the diners sit around the outside on stools, eating each dish as and when it's ready. It's an expensive way to go about cooking, with a dedicated chef to each table of diners, but you do eat the food freshly cooked, straight off the grill.

The chef revealed a beautiful, huge slab of light pinkish Kobe sirloin. He cut off one large steak, which his manager then weighed. I could swear I could see dollar signs in his eyes, but he tried to hide it. The chef poured a little oil on the grill, and patted the steak a little to make me think he was earning his cash, then basically quick-fried it for a minute and a half on each side. He chopped it into finger-size slices, put them on a plate, and slid them over to me.

The slices of beef didn't look particularly amazing—they just looked like well-grilled steak. But I put one in my mouth and I nearly fainted. It was like biting into a huge, overripe grape made of beef butter wrapped in ambrosia. It's soft, yet the fat is deliciously seared and caramelized, giving a little crust that contrasts with the velvety texture inside. As I felt the beef melt in my mouth, I could swear that choirs of angels sang Thomas Tallis' "Spem in Alium" (the most beautiful piece of music ever created) in my head, and I realized how lucky I was to have had such a rare and wonderful experience.

Kobe steaks are extremely well marbled with fat. Most of the flavor in the beef comes from its fat, but the trick with raising it is to get the fat into the muscles themselves in order to make the meat taste great, rather than losing it into pockets that are too much to eat on their own. Well, this particular cow had definitely managed to create the perfect balance.

Wagyu

Kobe refers to beef from the Tajima-ushi breed of Wagyu cattle raised in Hyogo Prefecture in Japan (the capital of which is the city of Kobe). There are strict rules involving the sake and beer diet, plus daily massages, but in fact although Wagyu translates as "Japanese cow," Wagyu cattle can be raised anywhere (there seems to be a growing market in New Zealand-raised Wagyu). Kobe is particularly renowned for the beef it produces. The Japanese Ministry of Agriculture hasn't taken very kindly to new producers, and it rejects any beef labeled "Wagyu" that has been bred outside Japan.

To drink: Highly refined Sake (one that uses highly polished rice)

㉖ Cooking with gold

Eating gold is an extraordinary and unforgettable experience. It's inert, tasteless, and very expensive, but it gives food a magic that you can't get any other way. You could say that it's also profligate and wasteful, but I think that would be missing the point. I'm not suggesting that you start chewing your wedding ring or roasting your swimming medals, but if there's something to celebrate, or perhaps you're feeling the need for a little sunshine in your life, well, what the hell?

You can eat gold without fear (although that wedding ring should be flattened into gold leaf first). When you eat it, gold goes straight through your digestive system and can't be metabolized, so it goes straight out again.

Gold crops up in wedding food in India and Pakistan (sometimes scattered in the rice) and is also found on candies across the world. Fine confectioners use little flakes of gold to jazz up their chocolates. I enjoy gilding unlikely things to add a little humor to the surprise—try gilding lemon slices for dropping into Christmas cocktails.

I find that the best gold to use for food is transfer leaf gold, which is available from any good artist's materials store. It works best when pressed against something that has a giving texture or is very slightly damp or greasy—sausages are good, as are scallops, poached fish, or cooked rice, You really want to get the highest quality 24-carat transfer leaf, otherwise you're buying an alloy cut with other metals, and I'm afraid I can't vouch for any of them. The gold has been beaten to the thickness of a few atoms, and isn't too expensive, considering the effect you're going to achieve.

Good foods for gilding:

Gelatin desserts: Lay it on when the gelatin has set, straight from the sheet of gold.

Cakes

Chocolate

Cheese

A note on Monsieur Mangetout

No discussion on the consumption of precious metals would be complete without a mention of this marvelous guy, who has racked up an impressive collection of vehicles that he has eaten, including a Cessna 150 aircraft. He eats about 2.4 lb/1 kilogram of material a day when performing one of his feats, and accompanies the odd material with oil and loads of water. Why he does this, I don't know. Perhaps it's so that he could be mentioned in books like this. Perhaps he just likes the taste of metal. Whatever the reason, I'm glad he does it.

To drink: Bols Gold Wasser de Danzig, a cinnamon and gold-leaf liqueur containing little floaty pieces of gold

㉗ Classic caviar

Much as I hate snobbery in food, there are rare occasions when it pays to bite your tongue and play by the rules of the elite. One of these occasions is when you've invested an absurd amount of money in a small can of fish eggs. I will never be able to afford enough caviar to be able to risk ruining it in some crazy culinary experiment. On the rare occasions that I can afford to buy caviar, I want to eat it in a way that will definitely work.

This is the classic way to serve caviar, as tried and tested by the richest people in the world. It may sound like an odd combination when you think that baked potatoes are so basic and cheap, but that's the whole point; you're serving caviar with simple flavors that don't interfere, but allow the caviar flavors to be drawn out and enjoyed as a whole dish rather than a single hit. By keeping the whites and yolks of the eggs separate, their flavor remains surprisingly delicate.

Each person is given a baked potato, and then puts a dollop of sour cream, a spoonful of egg white, and another of egg yolk on their plates. The caviar should be served straight from the can, just a little warmer than refrigerator temperature, and each person takes a spoonful of it, trying to take as much as possible, without looking greedy (you'll hear a lot of people squeak a little "oops, have I taken too much?" before swiftly passing on the can). You take a very lightly buttered potato topped with sour cream, then a little egg white and a little egg yolk, then the caviar is placed on the top. Some people prefer less egg so they get more of the caviar flavor.

ingredients

Serves 4 as a rich appetizer

8 small—medium baking potatoes

olive oil

4 eggs

2 oz/55 g canned sevruga, beluga, or osetra caviar (or as much as you can afford), chilled

1¹/₄ cups sour cream

To drink: A dry vintage pink Champagne. Well, why not?

The other way to eat caviar

Okay, there is one other way that the superrich like to take their caviar, and that's undiluted, eaten straight from a spoon. The problem is that a 1-oz/25-g can of caviar will last about 20 seconds this way. With the baked potato approach, you get the opportunity to enjoy and understand the caviar and its complex flavors.

Which caviar?

I'm talking about the real stuff here, you understand: The salted roe of the noble sturgeon, called sevruga, beluga, or osetra. There are others that are loads of fun to eat, and play with, such as the large bright orange eggs of the salmon, lumpfish caviar, which is excellent as a pasta sauce mixed with sour cream. But the real stuff is on another plane entirely: It has depth, a tremendous soft, yet membrous egglike texture and a light saltiness. There's also an undeniable frisson of pleasure (or is that guilt?) at the sheer unadulterated luxury of the experience.

Fake caviar

There is a bizarre caviar-esque substance available in some stores. I normally hate the idea of these artificial foods, but this stuff is intriguing and tastes pretty good. It's an odd, not-quite caviar substance made from seaweed, and has an extraordinary texture. It won't ever take the place of real caviar, but it's affordable and vegetarian, and is fun in pasta. Try it if you find some.

method

Preheat the oven to 400°F/200°C. Prick the potatoes lightly with a fork, then rub them with a little olive oil and place them in a single layer in a roasting pan. Place them in the preheated oven and bake for 45–60 minutes, then let cool for 15 minutes before serving.

While the potatoes are baking, place the eggs in a saucepan of water and bring to a boil. Simmer for 8 minutes, until hard-cooked. Let cool and then gently cut open so that the yolk remains intact. Separate the yolks and the whites, then grate each of them and place in separate bowls.

Take the caviar out of the refrigerator 5 minutes before serving, and place the whole can on a plate. Put the potatoes in a bowl, the sour cream in another bowl, and serve.

㉘ Oysters

You either love oysters or loathe them. I'll tell you right away that I love these bivalves with a passion that borders on the obsessive, but perhaps it would be useful to any oyster virgins if I start by describing them as dispassionately as possible.

Here goes: Once you have opened your oyster, everything you find inside is edible—unless you find a pearl (although in my many years of bivalve munching I never have). Oysters smell of the sea, which isn't surprising, as they come with a few spoonfuls of seawater firmly trapped in their shells, and the taste is difficult to describe—it's a little like eating sweet, solid seawater with the merest hint of shellfishy-ness, and the texture is both slippery and crunchy. For the squeamish among you, they don't really taste of fish, they don't smell fishy, and, although they are very much alive as you eat them, they don't wriggle as they go down. They are often eaten with a squeeze of lemon, a dash of Tabasco sauce, or some red wine vinegar mixed with some finely chopped shallots. This acidity works with the sweetness of the flesh and adds significantly to their flavor.

Oysters have become symbols of love, sex, decadence, and luxury, but I think that what makes them extra special is that magical little sense of anticipation when you eat them that this might just be the one that contains a pearl! Oysters fascinate me. My family still ridicule me for once forcing them to spend an entire baking-hot summer's day at a museum of oyster culture rather than on the adjacent beach. I haven't the foggiest idea what they were complaining about; that place was amazing, showing in exhaustive detail the history of the brave local oystermen and the techniques they developed to cement the oysters to the oyster ropes. Definitely good socio-gastronomico-cultural material for a two-year-old. Incidentally, my daughter Daisy ate her first oyster at the age of two, and although she hasn't developed an appetite for them that's quite as huge as mine, I can sense that it's only a matter of time.

To drink: A bone-dry Chablis

Cooking oysters

Many oyster aficionados sneer at the thought of cooking them, but although I love them raw, I do also enjoy them broiled briefly, topped with a dab of garlic and parsley butter, seasoning, and a covering of bread crumbs. They are also fantastic when placed in their half-shells on a grill. The smokiness of the charcoal flavors the oysters while they poach in their own seawater. Marvelous stuff.

Where to eat oysters

There is no bad place to eat oysters, as long as they are served shiveringly fresh and clean, but some restaurants throw an extra portion of joy into the experience. My favorite places to eat oysters: The oyster bar at Grand Central Station, the Royal Oyster House in Whitstable, Kent, England, and, possibly best of all, on the terrace of Les Jardins de la Mer restaurant in Bouziques in the south of France, overlooking the oyster lagoon of the Étang de Thau, and listening to the quirky tragicomic ballads of Georges Brassens. Oh. Mon. Dieu!

㉙ Pata Negra ham

I know that this is a book of superlatives, and that by their very nature, all of the dishes here are in some way spectacular, unique, or life-changing, but this is different. Pata Negra ham is a distillation of all the good things about food pulled apart and put back together in wafer-thin slivers. It is my favorite single food and it's—justfiably—cripplingly expensive. It's way too expensive for serving to your friends—share it between yourself and the love of your life.

Pata Negra (translates as "black hoof") ham comes from beautiful Black Iberian Pigs fattened on acorns in the cork oak groves on the border between Spain and Portugal. In Spain, it's called Jamon Iberico de Montanera or Jamon Iberico de Bellota. It has such an extraordinarily strong flavor and a startling depth that it feels like you can actually taste the craftsmanship and love that goes into making it. You'd be forgiven for suspecting that I get free ham from the producers in return for plugging their product, but nothing could be farther from the truth—every time I ask, they laugh in my face! The truth is that they don't need my help because all of their ham is sent straight to a select group of the world's finest delis.

I have to admit that it's not a dish in the traditional sense because there's no recipe here. In fact, the last thing you should do with Pata Negra ham is cook with it. That would be a tragedy along the lines of cooking with toro tuna, stewing caviar, or driving an Aston Martin DB8 at peak time. If you can't find Pata Negra ham in your deli, the best solution is to throw money at the problem: Buy the finest, most mature, most expensive Spanish ham you can find.

I always have a whole cured ham available in my kitchen (not Pata Negra, sadly). It sits in the corner on a rudimentary ham stand and I slice as needed, then cover it with a thin towel to prevent my cat from nibbling it. I have promised myself that one day when I have more money than I strictly need, I will buy myself a whole Pata Negra. I fear that day is still a long way off.

The Black Iberian Pig

This ancient breed of pig is highly active, with a huge appetite, eating around 40 lb/18 kg of acorns a day during the season. It also has a useful ability to grow huge quantities of fat under its skin and between its muscle fibers, and this seems to be the reason the ham is so good. Because the hams are salt-cured and then air-dried, moisture is extracted, leaving behind protein and fat and intensifying the flavor. The longer the ham is dried, the more intense the flavor, but the drier it becomes. With the Black Iberian Pig, the fat actually sits in the muscles themselves so the ham can be dried for a long time but still tastes moist and silky, with a powerful, intense flavor.

Serve this ham with...

Ice-cold Manzanilla sherry, home-toasted almonds, and padron chiles—about one in eight of these is hot, but it's impossible to tell which. It's like vegetable Russian roulette!

To drink: Manzanilla or dry Oloroso sherry

How to eat Pata Negra

Unwrap the ham and carefully lay it out on a plate. If it's been in the refrigerator, give it 10 minutes to warm to room temperature.

Pour yourself a glass of fine Manzanilla sherry.

Toss some almonds in sea salt, place them on a baking sheet, and broil them lightly.

Toss a bag of padron chiles in salt and a tiny amount of olive oil and then fry them until they just start to blacken.

Sit down. Give thanks. Eat.

I envy you.

㉚ Porcini with parsley & olive oil

These mushrooms are one of the great ingredients of all time—a fact that is sadly but fairly reflected in their price. They have an inimitable depth of flavor and rate alongside truffles as one of the few ingredients worth spending a king's ransom on in order to experience one of life's great sensual pleasures. They are large, solid-looking fungi with a white flesh and a large, almost cartoonishly mushroomlike cap. They look like a cross between a Champagne cork and a classic bread roll—their old English name is "Penny Bun."

This method of cooking them is called "à la Bordelaise," made famous by Alcide Bontou in his 1929 book *Traite de Cuisine Bourgeoise Bordelaise*, via Elizabeth David's *French Provincial Cooking*. It's still the best way to enjoy the full potential of porcini—there are loads of other recipes for them, but, as with truffles, simplicity and a firm resolve are required if you really want to enjoy their true flavor.

Foraging for your own porcini will save you a fortune, and they are relatively easy to identify from the huge variety of other dull or poisonous fungi. Always take a good mushroom-identity book with you if you pick your own, and check that you're not breaking the law or upsetting the owner of the land.

Dried porcini

Dried porcini are widely available—they dry really well, and retain a huge amount of their flavor, which intensifies as they dehydrate. They behave very differently from fresh mushrooms in cooking, but they are brilliant for risottos, and give a wonderful depth to stews, soups, and ragùs, where they can be dropped in dry. They can be added to any dish of cheap mushrooms to lift them to starrier flavor heights.

Fake porcini

I once bought some "Chinese porcini" in a market that were only one fifth of the price of the French ones in the next crate. I'm no food snob, and I didn't particularly care where my porcini came from. I sniffed them and they smelled nearly the same as the French ones, so I did what any self-respecting gastronaut might do—I bought all 15 lb/7 kg that the trader had. I took them home and invited over a gang of my best friends for a fungi frenzy and told them all to bring Champagne. They came. We drank. I cooked. Disaster! After cooking, the mushrooms tasted of absolutely nothing. It was like eating fibrous polystyrene. I felt well and truly humbled. Ever since then I have been extremely skeptical about any surprisingly cheap ingredients.

method

ingredients

Serves 4 as a large appetizer

1 lb/450 g firm porcini
generous ⅓ cup extra virgin olive oil
2 garlic cloves, finely chopped
large handful of parsley, chopped
salt and pepper
sourdough toast, to serve

Clean the porcini and separate the heads from the stalks. Chop the stalks roughly and set aside. Place a skillet over high heat and add the oil. When it's shimmering, add the porcini heads and fry. Check the undersides—when they have begun to brown, turn them over. Season with salt and pepper.

Add the garlic, chopped porcini stalks, and parsley and sauté for 5–10 minutes, until the flavors really start to release and the garlic's bite eases a little.

Serve on slices of sourdough toast with a drizzle of the hot olive oil from the pan.

To drink: A New World Pinot Noir, a spicy red wine

4. Restaurant classics

Restaurant classics

I go to restaurants to be taken on a sensual journey, to experience something I can't experience at home, achieved using ingredients and tools that aren't found in domestic kitchens. If I go to a restaurant and I haven't eaten something new, or tasted an unfamiliar combination, perhaps floated atop a pool of shimmering lights or tasted a dish cooked to a level of perfection that I can only dream about achieving myself, I wonder: What's the point? I can cook something more interesting, tastier, or more fascinating in the comfort of my own home for a fraction of the price charged in a restaurant.

Restaurants don't have to be expensive to deliver the goods; my regular haunt is a local Turkish "oçakbasi" restaurant that has an open charcoal grill in the middle of the room. It really is just a pile of charcoals, but over this unassuming half-spent fuel, a sullen, unsmiling Turkish chef wrings depths of flavor from lamb that make my own grill weep salty tears. In return for this wonderful sensual journey, the establishment charges the price of a bottle of a fancy restaurant's bottled water.

There are some dishes that I will happily admit are best eaten in restaurants: Fish with French fries, dishes involving spun sugar or octopus, and millefeuilles of anything. But the recipes in this chapter are all ones that can easily be transported home and faithfully recreated with the ordinary domestic *batterie de cuisine*. Once you've cooked them at home, you'll never look back.

It's interesting that many of the dishes in this chapter have a 1970s feel. Beef Wellington, Crown Roast of Lamb, and Saltimbocca all have their place in the world of nylon flares, but perhaps that's because they have been around forever, and it was only in the 1970s that I was aware of people starting to visit restaurants. These are old classics that have been fashionable, and perhaps have fallen out of fashion and been rediscovered. I love some history in a dish, especially when it's wearing flares.

There are dishes that sound complicated or scary, but are actually easy for you to make at home: Steak Tartare, Classic Roasted Duck Breast, and Saltimbocca. There are slightly more involved ones, such as Beef Wellington and Poule au Pot, and, of course, the familiar classic, Steak with Béarnaise Sauce, all of which cost an arm and a leg at a restaurant, where they have to charge you a portion of their rent, their dishwasher, their investors' expectations, their human resources, and the costs of the bus boy's light fingers.

I hope that this chapter will give you the confidence to make some dishes that up until now may have seemed to live in institutions. Let's you and me bust the locks and set them free from the chefs to enjoy them at home!

(31) Steak tartare

The habit of eating raw meat with raw egg and tart vinegar-based ingredients seems to have originated in Germany, but these days it's mostly seen on French restaurant menus.

The word "steak" comes from the Old Norse "steikjo," meaning to spit roast, but the word "tartare" is a reference to the allegedly bloodthirsty Turkic Tartars or "Tatars," who joined Genghis Khan's army as he was founding the Mongol Empire. Khan pursued an aggressive foreign policy and the Tatars were seen as bloodthirsty barbarians. So, for better or worse, their name was attached to the dish made of raw beef.

In case you haven't heard of this dish before, I'll be frank—it's a mixture of raw beef, raw egg, onions, capers, Tabasco sauce, and Worcestershire sauce. I know, I know, it sounds weird, but it's actually a fine, delicious, and magical combination.

Some people are often afraid of steak tartare because it's made with raw meat and eggs. Others only eat it in restaurants in fear of making it wrong at home. It's my job to rectify that, because it's ridiculously easy (and cheap, compared to the restaurant version) to make. In fact, it's probably better to make this at home, where you can be much more confident of kitchen hygiene—and because you are the one buying the beef, you can be absolutely sure that it's the highest quality. Just follow the usual rules (store raw meat on the bottom shelf of your refrigerator, use separate cutting boards for raw and cooked food, and keep your kitchen spotlessly clean) and you'll be fine.

When buying the meat, it's a good idea to mention to your butcher that you'll be using it for steak tartare, because he'll probably select a particularly choice cut for you. You should buy fine, well-aged steak but don't, whatever you do, ask the butcher to grind it for you—it needs to be cut by hand, not mangled! And don't be seduced by the succulent, bright red meat—that's likely to be young, tough, watery, and flavorless.

You may be surprised or appalled to learn that it is sometimes made with horsemeat, which is leaner than beef, and assumed to be healthier because horses are not affected by tuberculosis or tapeworms. In markets in the south of France, you can still find "chevalines"— butchers dealing in horsemeat—and they are very popular.

ingredients

Serves 4 as a main course

1 lb 2 oz/500 g excellent-quality beef
tenderloin or sirloin steak

2 tbsp parsley, finely chopped

2 tbsp capers, finely chopped

2 tbsp shallots, finely chopped

2 tbsp gherkins, finely chopped

4 dashes Tabasco sauce

4 dashes Worcestershire sauce

2 tbsp Dijon mustard

1 tsp fine salt

4 egg yolks (kept separate)

French fries or boiled potatoes, to serve

method

Make sure all the ingredients, cutting board,
and mixing bowl are kept chilled—put them in
the refrigerator for 20 minutes before you start
preparing and take them out when ready to use.

Finely chop the beef by hand. Take your time, and
don't mush the beef or it will lose its texture and
seep all its juices. Lay the meat in the chilled bowl.
Add all the remaining ingredients, except the egg
yolks, and mix them into the beef with a fork.

Shape the mixture into four round patties and
make an indent in the middle of each. Place in the
refrigerator until ready to serve.

When you are ready to serve, place each patty
in the middle of a plate and lay an egg yolk in
the indent.

Serve with French fries and tell your guests to mix
the egg yolk into the beef.

To drink:
Iced Bison Grass vodka

㉜Beef Wellington

There's a lot of fantastic history surrounding this very British dish, but first let's concentrate on how great it tastes. It's basically a piece of fine beef wrapped in a mixture of mushrooms, pâté, Madeira, and, sometimes, truffles, and then wrapped in a crust of light puff pastry and baked. You'd expect it to taste good, really, because it's made using tenderloin, the best and most expensive cut of beef. But there's more to it than that. The cooking method is *en croûte* (in crust), and the layer of pâté and mushrooms that lies between the meat and the puff pastry ensures that secondary cooking happens extremely gently and evenly.

I won't try to deceive you. This dish takes a while to prepare—between 1 and 2 hours, depending on how adept you are in the kitchen—but it's a refined, sumptuous, and grown-up meal that serves a lot of people. You probably wouldn't rustle this up on a school night for the kids, but if you've got some good friends or family coming around who appreciate the finer things in life, and who you'd like to pamper, I thoroughly recommend spending a couple of hours immersed in foodie heaven making this.

Wellington

It's tempting to think that the name of this dish refers to the British rubber boots, as though the pastry wraps itself around the beef like a boot, but it's more likely that this was named after Arthur Wellesley, the First Duke of Wellington, one of the great British military figures of the eighteenth century, and thought by some to be one of the greatest generals of all time. He defeated Napoleon at Waterloo, and served as prime minister of Britain twice. No one's sure if the dish was invented for him or if it was just named after him. It was also the favorite dish of another British prime minister, Sir Winston Churchill.

To drink:
Crozes Hermitage red wine

ingredients

Serves 6 as a main course

2 tbsp olive oil or vegetable oil

3 lb 5 oz/1.5 kg beef tenderloin, cut from the middle of the tenderloin, trimmed of fat and sinew

5 tbsp butter

$2^{1}/_{4}$ cups chopped mushrooms

2 garlic cloves, crushed

5 oz/150 g smooth liver pâté

few drops of truffle oil (optional)

1 tbsp fresh parsley, finely chopped

2 tsp English mustard

1 lb 2 oz/500 g puff pastry

1 egg, lightly beaten

salt and pepper

wilted greens and roasted root vegetables, including parsnips, to serve

method

Place a large skillet over high heat and add the oil. Rub salt and pepper into the beef and sear very quickly all over in the skillet. (This method creates a rare version. If you want it less rare, roast it at 425°F/220°C for 20 minutes at this stage.) Set aside to cool.

Heat the butter in a skillet over medium heat, add the mushrooms, and fry for 5 minutes. Reduce the heat, add the garlic, and fry for an additional 5 minutes. Put the mushrooms and garlic in a bowl, add the pâté, truffle oil, if using, and parsley, and beat with a fork. Let cool.

Rub the mustard into the seared beef. Roll out the pastry into a rectangle that is large enough to wrap the whole tenderloin with some to spare. Spread the mushroom paste in the middle of the pastry in a shape the size of the bottom of the beef and lay the beef on top. Brush the edges of the pastry with beaten egg and fold it over, edges overlapping, and across the meat to completely enclose it.

Preheat the oven to 425°F/200°C. Place the wrapped beef in a roasting pan with the seam underneath and brush with beaten egg. Let chill in the refrigerator for 15 minutes, then transfer to the preheated oven and bake for 50 minutes. Check after 30 minutes—if the pastry looks golden brown, cover it in foil to prevent it from burning.

Serve with wilted greens and roasted root vegetables.

In the recipe graveyard in the sky lives a whole subclass of embarrassing but wonderful meals that were laid to rest because they became uncool. You know the ones I'm talking about: Lobster thermidor, cheese fondue, coq au vin, and anything cooked in lard. Some dishes have been consigned to food history: Gruel and corn mash (may they rest in peace). Crown Roast of Lamb is the grandpa of them all, sporting those 1970s mini chef's hats. This isn't just culinary nostalgia (although I have been known to indulge a little) but a real celebration of a wonderful dish.

③ Crown roast of lamb

This classic 1970s stylish dinner party dish is all about the wonderful rack of lamb—it is expensive, tender, and delicious, with the lean noisette of meat running through it and, when cooked properly, it's as refined as lamb ever gets. When you buy these expensive cuts, you find that there's relatively little cooking involved (I often find myself wandering around my kitchen looking for something to do when I make this).

I'm tempted to say that those little white chef's hats are optional, but perhaps as a mark of respect, you should see them as compulsory. You can actually still buy them from catering stores, but maybe it would be more fun to get your kids to make them?

ingredients

Serves 4 as a main course

2 x 4-rib racks of lamb, fat trimmed (but not removed) and bones trimmed of membrane

olive oil

3 sprigs thyme

large glass of Marsala or white wine

2 tbsp water

1 tsp red currant sauce

pat of butter

salt and pepper

To serve

sautéed potatoes

minted peas

method

Preheat the oven to 425°F/220°C. Remove the lamb from the refrigerator. Lightly oil the racks all over, then rub salt and pepper into the fat and flesh using your fingers. Lay the two racks against each other in a roasting pan, ribs interlocking, skin on the outside. Slip the thyme in between the racks and wrap some foil around the bones at the end of the ribs to prevent them from burning.

Place in the preheated oven and roast for 15 minutes, then reduce the oven temperature to 325°F/160°C and roast for an additional 15 minutes (this will give you a nice pink meat—if you prefer it well done, cook for 25 minutes). Remove from the oven and let rest (reserving the thyme and juices in the pan) while you make some gravy.

Pour off any excess fat from the roasting pan. If the thyme has burned, discard and add another 2 sprigs, then add the Marsala, water, and red currant sauce and stir. Place over medium heat and simmer for 10 minutes, until reduced by half. Stir in the butter.

Put little chef's hats on the bones (oh, go on), then carve it (at the table, naturally) into individual chops and serve with sautéed potatoes and minted peas.

To drink: Pinot Noir— New World or Austrian, if you can find it

㉞ Pan-fried sea bass with gently garlicked pommes puree

This is one of those classic restaurant dishes that, once found on a menu, have an almost irresistible gravitational force, making it hard to order anything else. It's refined yet comforting, healthy yet filling. And, of course, it always helps to have an adjective in the title.

Sea bass is one of my favorite fish because it's got a robust, full flavor and a skin that, if cooked right, is a joy to eat. It also has a firm texture, so it cooks well. For all these reasons, plus the fact that it's relatively expensive to buy, it's one of those fish like gilt-headed bream or halibut that shouldn't be fooled about with. You want it to express its own flavor, not that of a curry or of herbs, so you don't need to do anything special to it other than treat it with respect. The gently garlicked pommes puree are a perfect accompaniment, acting both as a sauce and a bed for the fish.

Note: The pommes puree are best done with a potato ricer to achieve the smoothness.

Sea bass

The French call bass loup de mer (sea wolf) because it's a voracious predator with a huge appetite. It's an accomplished hunter and, as it gets older, it becomes more and more solitary. This fish has been revered for its flavor and tenderness for centuries. It's silvery, with tight scales, and grows up to 3 feet/90 cm in length, although the largest I've ever met was about 2 feet/60 cm. It was mentioned by Pliny in the first century AD and remains expensive and highly prized, despite the relatively recent development of cheap farmed bass.

ingredients

Serves 4 as a main course

1 lb 12 oz/800 g large potatoes, peeled

6 whole garlic cloves, unpeeled

generous $^3/_4$ cup milk

generous $^1/_3$ cup heavy cream

5 tbsp butter, cubed

4 x 7 oz/200 g sea bass fillets,
scaled but not skinned

3 tbsp olive oil

salt and pepper

minted peas or a crunchy salad, to serve

**To drink: An unoaked
Chardonnay**

method

Cut the potatoes into walnut-size chunks. Fill a large saucepan with cold water, add some salt and the potatoes, and bring to a boil. Simmer the potatoes for 10–15 minutes, until tender, then drain and return to the pan. Heat and stir for an additional 2 minutes to dry them out. Mash them using a potato ricer (a potato masher won't really make them smooth enough) and set aside in the warm pan.

Bring a small saucepan of water to a boil, add the garlic, and blanch for 2 minutes, then drain and run it under a little cold water. Peel off the skins and mash the garlic using a garlic crusher or the back of a spoon. Mix this into the potato.

Put the milk in a saucepan and heat until hot but not boiling, then stir it into the potato, along with the cream. Heat this over low heat for about 5 minutes, adding the butter a cube at a time. The potato should have a smooth consistency like a thick mayonnaise. Cover and keep warm.

Carefully score the skin of the fish with a few diagonal cuts, being careful not to cut the flesh. Season with salt and pepper. Pour the oil into a large skillet and place over medium–high heat until shimmering. Fry the fillets, skin-side down, for 4 minutes. Check that the skin is crispy, then turn carefully and fry on the other side for just 1 minute.

Spread some potato in the center of four warmed plates and place a fish fillet on top, skin-side up. Serve with minted peas.

③⑤ Frog's legs

Most people think that frog's legs and snails are comedy food. A parody of French cuisine, perhaps, or an example of the outer limits of gastronomy that really don't need to be explored, thank you very much.

This is a shame because frog's legs are really good, although I have to admit that I've begun to give up on snails. They don't really have much flavor to them, other than the pool of garlic and butter they tend to sit in. They have an interesting texture, but are too expensive for what they are.

Frog's legs, however, are a different story because they are delicious and tender, and have a unique character. The meat is sweet and succulent and they are actually pretty easy to cook. I'll admit to having a freezer full of them right now, bought from my local fish dealer (they are amphibians, not fish, but who's complaining?).

If you manage to lay your hands on some of these delicate little beauties, they are probably frozen, having been shipped from either France or Southeast Asia. They are, like soft-shelled crabs, usually individually wrapped in little plastic sheets so that they don't turn into a single solid froggy block.

How to cook frog's legs

If the legs were frozen, make sure that they have been thoroughly thawed. Pat them dry with paper towels, then season with salt and pepper. Pour two handfuls of all-purpose flour into a bowl, add a couple of crushed garlic cloves, some more salt and pepper, and some fresh thyme leaves. Toss the frog's legs in the flour. Heat a skillet over medium–high heat and add a large pat of butter. When it's beginning to brown, add the legs and fry until crispy, then turn over and fry again. Season with salt and pepper, and eat them as if they were small chicken drumsticks.

What do they taste like?

It always annoys me when people say that unfamiliar meat probably tastes "a little like chicken." I always like to say that walrus, rat, weevils, and frog's legs all taste a little as you'd expect walrus, rat, weevils, and frog's legs to taste. Frog's legs don't taste at all fishy, as you might expect—they taste like tender, soft quails' wings. Okay—a little bit like young chicken. But the flesh seems sweeter and more tender and, if you close your eyes and think hard, just a little bit—froggy.

To drink: An arrogant French Chardonnay

36 Classic roasted duck breast with sweet red currant sauce

Duck stuff

My favorite duck is the Indian Runner, which is a great layer, producing up to 200 eggs a year. It has a wonderful, snooty bearing, and does, indeed, look as if it is running around in a hurry, holding neck and body bolt upright as it moves. Indian Runners are called ducklings up to the age of about six months.

This is one of those wonderful dishes that is often seen on restaurant menus, but these days is rarely cooked in the home. It's a great shame, and I'm not entirely sure why this has come about. Perhaps it's because duck breast is a relatively expensive ingredient, so people are wary in case they make a mistake and waste it.

The most important thing to remember is that duck breast, unlike chicken, is fantastic when served rare. You need to be careful when searing and rendering the fat, but other than that, you don't need to be a trained chef to cook this. Another great advantage of duck breast is that it will carry a strong, fruity sauce.

The dish duck à l'orange may have become a byword for unfashionable, but I have a deep fondness for it. It was exactly the sort of food served in all the restaurants my family could never afford to eat in. I would gaze longingly at the menus and later I'd try to imagine what those exotic-sounding dishes might taste like while I ate much cheaper food elsewhere.

To drink: A nice big red Rioja

ingredients

Serves 4 as a substantial main course

4 duck breasts, skin on
$^{1}/_{2}$ tbsp vegetable oil
4 shallots, finely chopped
2 garlic cloves, crushed
2 tbsp fresh thyme leaves
generous $^{3}/_{4}$ cup red wine
4 tbsp sherry or balsamic vinegar
6 tbsp red currant jelly
5 tbsp butter, cut into chunks
salt and pepper

To serve

Roast Potatoes (see page 113), or mashed
potatoes
watercress salad
glazed carrots

method

NOTE: Once you have started to cook this recipe, everything should happen in the space of 30–45 minutes, so make sure you have prepared all the ingredients beforehand.

Preheat the oven to 350°F/180°C. Score the skin of each duck breast with four diagonal cuts down to the fat (but not into the meat). Season with salt and pepper. Place a large, heavy-bottom skillet over high heat, add the oil, then add the duck breasts, skin-side down. Sear for about 10 minutes, until the skin is crisp. Be careful, because they will spit. Turn the breasts over and sear on the other side for 2 minutes. Remove from the skillet and put into a roasting pan. Keep warm.

Pour off most of the fat from the skillet, reserving about a tablespoon. Put the skillet over medium heat, add the shallots, and fry for 5–10 minutes, until softened. Meanwhile, put the duck breast into the preheated oven and cook for about 15 minutes (this will cook the duck to pink, which is how it should be served). Add the garlic and thyme to the skillet and cook for an additional 2 minutes. Add the wine and vinegar, simmer for 5 minutes, then stir in the red currant jelly and butter. When the duck is cooked, remove it from the oven, cover, and keep warm for 5 minutes.

Cut each breast diagonally into five fat slices, lay on warmed plates, and pour over the sauce. Serve with roast potatoes, watercress salad, and glazed carrots.

37 Soupe de poissons with rouille

You could call this "fish soup," but I think that would lose a little of the magic. Despite its name, this really isn't a refined dish. In fact, it's exactly the opposite—a robust, rustic, peasant dish—often made out of the flotsam and jetsam of a good fish meal. The flavor is rich and strong, and I must admit that I often enjoy this dish made from the remnants of good fish more than the fish themselves.

The best soupe de poissons I ever made used the parts and shards of crabs that I swept off the table after I'd had a Crab & Stone Party (see page 28) and I was too tired to throw it all away. It was a bisque, really (see recipe opposite). I've even made a fabulous version of this with a saucepan full of shrimp shells after cooking Easy, Finger-Licking Garlicky Shrimp (see page 196). Mind-blowing stuff.

To cook this well you don't need skill—you need attitude. It needs to be cooked roughly and crudely, and you have to bully the flavor out of the bones by whacking and cracking them with a hammer or masher. You can use your food processor, but I tend to see this dish as an opportunity for a little anger management. Be bold!

Don't use...

oily fish, such as herring, mackerel, or salmon, which are no good for this dish.

Bisque micro-recipe

You don't need expensive ingredients for this—just 2 lb 4 oz/1 kg or so of cooked shellfish shells (or whole small crabs) from crabs, shrimp, and langoustine. In a large saucepan fry some chopped celery, carrots, onion, and bay leaves for 15 minutes, add a glass of wine or Vermouth, the shells or whole crabs, a can of tomatoes, and 6 cups of water. Bring to a boil and simmer for 30 minutes. Crush and mash the shells with a potato masher or hammer until they are as small as you can get them, then let the mixture stand for 20 minutes. Strain through a colander, then through a fine strainer and discard the shells. Add some cream, lemon juice, and pepper and serve with crusty bread.

ingredients

Serves 6–8 as an appetizer

generous ⅓ cup olive oil

3 onions, roughly chopped

3 carrots, roughly chopped

3 celery stalks, roughly chopped

1 fennel bulb, finely chopped

6 garlic cloves, roughly chopped

1 bay leaf

⅔ cup Vermouth

2 sprigs thyme

2 lb 4 oz/1 kg whole whitefish, cleaned and filleted, bones reserved

4 lb 8 oz/2 kg bones from whitefish or shellfish

9 oz/250 g unpeeled shrimp

11¼ cups water

juice and zest of 1 orange

pinch of saffron

toasted slices of baguette and grated Parmesan cheese, to serve

Rouille

½ cup fresh bread crumbs soaked in 1 tbsp water

3 garlic cloves, roughly chopped

1 egg yolk

1 red chile, seeded and chopped

½ tsp salt

generous ¾ cup olive oil

method

Place a large saucepan over medium heat and add the olive oil. Add the onions, carrots, celery, fennel, garlic, and bay leaf and cook gently for 20 minutes, until softened. Add the Vermouth and thyme and simmer for 2 minutes.

Add the fish, fish bones, and shrimp and increase the heat. Cook, stirring, for 5 minutes, then add the water, orange juice and zest, and saffron. Bring to a boil and simmer for 45 minutes.

Meanwhile, make the rouille. Put all of the ingredients except the olive oil into a food processor and blend to a paste. Keep blending and add the olive oil in a slow stream until the consistency is that of a nice thick mayonnaise. Put in the refrigerator to chill.

Crush the bones by liquidizing the soup in batches (yes, bones, shells, and all), or by using a potato masher and hammer in the saucepan. Let stand for 20 minutes. Strain through a colander first, then through a fine strainer, then pour into a saucepan. Taste and season and heat again, ready to serve.

Serve in bowls with slices of toasted baguette, bowls of rouille, and some grated Parmesan cheese to float on the soup.

To drink: A crisp, strong rosé wine

③⑧ Classic poule au pot

This classic stuffed, poached chicken dish has become criminally overlooked and is in urgent need of resurrection. It's a real spectacle, a two-course meal that's cooked in a single pot. Yes, you read it right: One pot to heat, one pot to fill, and, more importantly, one pot to wash up. It's not lazy cooking, because you do need to make some stuffing (it's a trial, I know), but it's well worth the effort. Oh, and that one pot does need to be large, because it's holding enough food for six hungry people.

This is the famous dish that made the sixteenth-century King Henry IV of Navarre, France, declaim "God willing, every working man in my kingdom will have a chicken in the pot every Sunday." Henry was a pretty decent guy, bringing peace and relative prosperity to France, and breaking the regal mold, showing that he cared about the ordinary man, so his vote counts for a lot.

The list of ingredients looks long, but they are all pretty cheap, simple foods. Of course, poule au pot is best when you use a happy free-range chicken, and these don't come cheap, but bear in mind that this method of cooking will also do wonders for an older, tougher bird.

To drink: Pouilly-Fuissé (French Chardonnay)

ingredients

Serves 6 as an appetizer and main course

6 cups chicken stock

6 cups water

bouquet garni of 4 sprigs parsley, 4 sprigs thyme, and 4 bay leaves tied with string

1 tsp black peppercorns

$5^1/_2$ oz/150 g smoked bacon, chopped into chunks

1 whole garlic bulb, halved

3 small leeks, trimmed and cut into large chunks

3 carrots, peeled and cut into large chunks

3 celery stalks, cut into large chunks

3 turnips, peeled and cut into large chunks

6 small onions

1 chicken, 4 lb 8 oz–5 lb 8 oz/2–2.5 kg

1 small head cabbage, cut into 6 pieces

12 small new potatoes, scrubbed

salt and pepper

Stuffing

$2^1/_4$ cups fresh bread crumbs

$4^1/_2$ oz/125 g chicken livers, finely chopped

1 shallot, finely chopped

1 egg

handful of parsley, finely chopped

$4^1/_2$ oz/125 g sausage meat

3 garlic cloves, crushed

$^1/_2$ tsp salt

pepper

Sauce

$4^1/_2$ oz/125 g gherkins, finely chopped

4 tbsp extra virgin olive oil

1 tbsp Dijon mustard

method

Take a very large saucepan and add the stock, water, bouquet garni, peppercorns, bacon, and all the vegetables, except the potatoes and cabbage, and season with salt and pepper. Bring to a very gentle simmer.

Meanwhile, put all the stuffing ingredients in a bowl and mix thoroughly. Season the cavity of the chicken with salt and pepper. Spoon in the stuffing and truss the chicken closed with string. Place in the pan with the stock, cover, and simmer very, very gently for

$1^1/_2$ hours. Add the cabbage and potatoes, bring back to a boil, and simmer for an additional 20 minutes.

Combine all the sauce ingredients in a bowl and mix well. Remove the chicken from the pan, wrap in foil, and let rest. Check the seasoning, then ladle the broth into bowls and serve as an appetizer.

Carve the chicken and serve on a plate with the vegetables and broth and the sauce on the side.

39 New York steak with Béarnaise sauce

What is a New York steak?

This steak is also known as a strip steak or shell steak, and it's a high-quality, high-cost piece of beef from a muscle that does little work, so it's extremely tender. It's usually well-marbled with fat so that it performs extremely well when pan-fried or broiled. It's particularly prone to overcooking.

Ah, yes, the carnivore's French bistro delight—perfect steak with Béarnaise sauce. There is an art to cooking a good steak, but it's an art that's easily learned, so stick with me. We're looking at one of the finest, most expensive slabs of meat available, so it would be a tragedy to get it wrong. And yet I've lost count of the amount of times I've been served disappointing, chewy, flavorless, overcooked steak in restaurants. And I know that some people (including my mother) insist on eating steaks cooked well done, but they really shouldn't be doing this with New York steak, because it's a waste.

There are several common causes of disappointing steaks:

1. Overcooking
2. Broiling temperature too low
3. Overcooking
4. Lack of proper resting
5. Overcooking
6. Not removing the steaks from the refrigerator for long enough before cooking
7. Overcook...you get the picture.

The ideal accompaniments to this dish are sautéed potatoes and salad. French fries would be good, but they may take a little too much concentration when you are tackling the Béarnaise!

ingredients

Serves 4 as a main course

4 New York steaks, or entrecôte,
8 oz/225 g each

1 tbsp olive oil (not virgin, because this will
burn) or clarified butter

salt and pepper

sautéed potatoes or French fries, to serve

Béarnaise sauce

large bunch of tarragon

1 shallot, finely chopped

generous $1/3$ cup white wine vinegar

4 peppercorns

2 egg yolks

$3/4$ cup butter, cut into small cubes

method

Remove the steaks from the refrigerator 20 minutes before you
intend to cook them.

To make the Béarnaise sauce, remove the most tender leaves
of the tarragon, finely chop, and set aside. Roughly chop the
tougher parts and add them to a small saucepan with the
shallot, vinegar, and peppercorns and simmer until it has
reduced to about 1 tablespoonful. Pass this through a strainer
into a clean heatproof bowl.

Bring a small saucepan of water to a boil, place the bowl
on top, and gently whisk in the egg yolks until the mixture
thickens a little. Add the butter a piece at a time and whisk it in
until the sauce is thick. Add the chopped tarragon leaves and
mix in. Taste and add salt if needed. Turn off the heat and cover
to keep warm while you cook the steaks.

Preheat the broiler to high with the broiler pan underneath,
Season the steaks with salt and pepper and brush with the oil.
Place the steaks on the preheated pan and cook quickly for 3–4
minutes on each side. Check that they are nicely seared, then
cover and let rest for 2 minutes before serving.

Stir the sauce in case it has separated. Serve the steaks on lightly
warmed plates with potatoes and the sauce spooned over.

To drink: A beautiful, gentle, and rich Pomerol (from Bordeaux, France)

⑩ Saltimbocca

Saltimbocca: What a beautiful word. I loved the sound of this dish a long time before I knew that it meant "jumps in the mouth" in Italian. It's a simple combination of thin chicken, pork, or veal wrapped in ham and rolled up around a sage leaf. The rolls are seared in butter and then poached in a splash of Marsala or white wine, and that's it. Classic Italian simplicity.

The most famous version of this dish is Saltimbocca alla Romana, the Roman version made with veal, but it's fantastic made with pork chops or pork tenderloin and chicken breast.

Buying prosciutto

Prosciutto is the Italian for all ham, although we've come to know it as referring specifically to prosciutto crudo: Raw, air-cured ham. These hams are made all over Italy, but the most famous are Parma ham (with a slightly nutty flavor from the cheese whey the pigs often eat) and San Daniele (with a distinctly sweet taste). The odd-sounding but fine-tasting speck is flavored with juniper and smoked before drying, and coppa isn't really a ham at all, but is made with rolled bacon, which produces a wonderful flavor and texture, but a fair amount of fat (go on—treat yourself). On the other hand, bresaola isn't ham at all—it's cured beef, dark and strongly flavored, and it's a wonderful antipasto.

Lardo

I LOVE lardo. It's wrong, being pure, cured pork fat, often rolled in crushed pepper, but it has a spectacular taste and texture. If you find some, ask for it to be cut as thinly as possible so that it looks translucent, then keep it next to something cold, otherwise it will be a devil to separate when you get it home. Lay it on a plate with the slices curled around so that they don't glue themselves down, then scatter large salt crystals over, some pepper, and a sprinkling of fresh rosemary leaves. Drizzle over a little fine olive oil (I know, I know—stick with me) and serve. It's delicious, and you get a sensation of eating outrageously soft, pure, edible silk.

ingredients

Serves 4 as a main course

4 pork chops, bones and fat removed

4 large, thin slices Parma ham or
San Daniele ham

4 large sage leaves

scant $\frac{1}{2}$ cup unsalted butter

generous $\frac{3}{4}$ cup Marsala, Madeira, or dry white
wine

salt and pepper

sautéed potatoes and a green salad, to serve

method

Lay the pork chops on a cutting board and flatten them with a mallet or rolling pin until they are the same size as the ham slices. Lay down a piece of ham, put a piece of pork on top, and place a sage leaf at the edge nearest to you. Season with salt and pepper, then roll the meat around the sage leaf and secure it with a toothpick. The ham should be on the outside. Repeat with the remaining chops.

Place a wide, heavy-bottom saucepan over high heat. Add the butter and then the meat rolls and brown them quickly on all sides. Add the Marsala and reduce the heat to a simmer. Cover and cook for about 10–15 minutes, until the meat is cooked through. Remove the rolls and keep them warm, and increase the heat to reduce the liquid for 2 minutes to thicken.

Serve the rolls on warmed plates with sautéed potatoes and a green salad and pour over a little of the sauce.

To drink: A good South
African Pinotage

5. International classics

International classics

Oh, if only I could have another thousand or so pages in which to describe the wondrous culinary adventures I've been treated to around the world. But inevitably this book is about drawing a line under the top 101 dishes and setting the lions loose on the rest of 'em. This chapter has been the most difficult in the entire book to limit to ten clear favorites, partly because I keep very detailed diaries and photojournals of my journeys, and every dish I've eaten ends up packed with a trunk of memories of extraordinary people I've met and places I've seen.

There are 193 countries that are generally recognized as independent states around the world (although, confusingly, there are 245 different countries if you include unrecognized and disputed states and dependent territories). All of these have their own proud culinary traditions, so choosing just ten of these for this chapter is bound to leave out some fantastic dishes. The ones I've chosen here are some of the most distinctive to me, or ones that have a particularly important history.

Of all the international cuisines I've tried, the most memorable has to be Chinese. It's not always the most refined or fancy, but it has a spectacular range, from roasted insects and grilled snake skins, to yak's penis and fish bladders. Don't worry, though. I've chosen the more palatable and easily sourced classic Peking Duck for you to try. It's another of my favorites because it's interactive: You do all the cooking, but everyone assembles their own little pancakes, and there's a little bit of magic to that act of creation.

This chapter has a huge range of wildly different flavors, from the fresh zest and citrus tang of Ceviche, to the heady spicing of whole Tandoori Chicken, and these are the deep, sexy, palate-tickling flavors that take you on a real global tour.

Inevitably, there are many dishes from Europe here, but I've chosen not to indulge the traditions of Escoffier and Carême and the more refined French classics, mainly because so many of them crop up in the other chapters of this book. Instead, I've opted for the rough and ready Rillettes, a simple rustic French dish that seems to me to capture everything that's good about provincial French food. The glory of Italian food has been boiled down here into Osso Buco, a dish that sings of the best of simple honest cooking from fine, cheap, decent ingredients.

I must admit to a deep, thoroughly biased fondness for roast beef with all the familiar British trimmings: Yorkshire pudding and horseradish sauce. When I was growing up we rarely, if ever, ate this using the properly expensive rib roast that makes it into a transcendentally good Sunday lunch, so it was at a relatively late stage in my life that I realized how good it could be. I am now a complete convert, and nothing makes me feel so warm and comfortable in my skin as a proper Sunday lunch like this, whenever budget allows.

So I thank the world for giving up its plenty and for the 6.7 billion other people who live in it, eating, cooking, and experimenting with everything that grows or roams on its soil, wrangling flavors and tastes and textures into their unique cultures and traditions.

㊶ Whole roast rib of beef (with Yorkshire pudding and everything!)

This is in my top ten dishes, without a doubt. It's the big British Sunday lunch eaten with all the family, and the table is expected to be heaving with roast potatoes, Yorkshire puddings, glazed carrots, steamed greens, and horseradish sauce. I must admit that I am actually salivating as I write these words, safe in the knowledge that I will be cooking the recipe opposite this very weekend.

The French tease the British, calling them "rosbifs," which is a) grammatically clumsy, b) a childish retort to the equally childish British habit of calling the French "frogs," and c) just fine, because if they haven't discovered how glorious a well-roasted rib of beef can be, that leaves more for me!

When you look at the recipe, you might think that the cooking time is a little short, and may even be tempted to cook the beef for longer. Don't. If you don't like rare meat, I strongly advise that you don't make this dish, as you'll be sorely disappointed by both the food and the large amount of cash you paid for it. This is a dish to eat rare or not at all.

ingredients

Serves 8 as a main course

6 lb 8-oz/3-kg joint of well-hung rib of beef
on the bone
olive oil
$^{1}/_{2}$ tbsp all-purpose flour
generous $^{3}/_{4}$ cup strong chicken stock
generous $^{3}/_{4}$ cup red wine
salt and pepper

Yorkshire pudding

$1^{3}/_{4}$ cups all-purpose flour, sifted
6 eggs
$^{1}/_{2}$ tsp salt
$2^{1}/_{2}$ cups milk
2 tbsp vegetable oil or lard

Roast potatoes

4 lb 8 oz/2 kg potatoes, peeled
6 tbsp sunflower oil or goose or duck fat
salt and pepper

To serve

glazed carrots
steamed broccoli
horseradish sauce
mustard

To drink: Crozes Hermitage

method

For the Yorkshire pudding, mix the flour, eggs, and salt together in a bowl, then gradually add the milk as you stir with a whisk. When smooth set aside but don't chill.

For the roast potatoes, bring a large saucepan of lightly salted water to a boil, add the potatoes, return to a boil, and cook for 10 minutes. Drain the potatoes and toss them in oil and salt and pepper. Put them in a roasting pan in a single layer.

Preheat the oven to 425°F/220°C. Put a 16 x 10-inch/ 40 x 25-cm roasting pan in the bottom of the oven to warm for the Yorkshire puddings.

Rub a generous amount of olive oil and salt and pepper into the beef, then place in a roasting pan. Transfer to the preheated oven and roast for 30 minutes. Reduce the temperature to 325°F/160°C. Transfer the potatoes to the oven and roast with the beef for 60 minutes. Remove the beef from the oven and increase the temperature to 425°F/220°C. Cover the beef with foil and let rest for at least 30 minutes.

Remove the roasting pan from the bottom of the oven and add the oil. Put it back in the oven for 5 minutes, then remove it and add the Yorkshire pudding batter. Put it back in the hot oven for about 20 minutes.

Meanwhile, make the gravy. Stir the flour into the leftover juices in the pan, add the stock and wine, then simmer over medium heat, until reduced by about half.

Remove the Yorkshire pudding and the potatoes from the oven. Cut the rib bones off the beef and carve the meat. Serve with the potatoes, Yorkshire pudding, carrots, broccoli, horseradish sauce, and mustard.

42 Crispy Peking duck

This is a delicious combination of light, crispy skin, succulent tender meat, and a deep, deep marinade flavoring. It particularly excites me because it's another of those interactive meals where each person assembles their own dinner, making rolled pancakes filled with a little meat, a dab of sauce, and a few scallions.

I used to think that Peking Duck was an otherworldly, complex meal that requires ancient expertise, strange ingredients, and arcane tools, but it's just not true. The ingredients are now widely available, and although you could build a mud-lined oven suspended on chains from your ceiling, you can get wonderful results from an average kitchen. The duck is marinated in hoisin sauce and honey. You'll need to do this overnight to get the right effect, but it's well worth the effort. I have unashamedly suggested that you buy store-bought hoisin sauce and pancakes to make your life easy.

Where to eat Peking Duck

Across the vast expanses of China, there's one word that strikes fear into all ducks: "Quanjude," and for good reason. The Quanjude restaurant in Beijing is generally accepted, by those who think about this sort of thing to be the global center of Peking Duck consumption. Abandon hope all ducks who enter here. Walk in, and once you've adjusted your eyes to the glare of miles of bright red polyester curtains, carpet, and tablecloths, you'll see that it's a wall-to-wall duckfest. The chef brings the bird to your table and majestically carves it into 60 separate pieces.

Play the finger game

It's traditional to play this game during a Peking Duck feast. Choose someone to play against. Think of a number between 0 and 10 and, after "ready, steady, go!" both players hold up one hand, with a random number of fingers extended, at the same time shouting out the guessed total number. The person who guesses the correct total of extended fingers wins, and the loser has to pay a forfeit, usually a drink. Be careful, though—this game can get both addictive and inebriated!

ingredients

Serves 6 as a main course

1 duck, 4 lb 8 oz–5 lb/2–2.5 kg

3 tbsp honey

$^2/_3$ cup hoisin sauce, or plum sauce, plus extra
to serve

splash of warm water

To serve

about 30 "Peking Duck" or
"Mandarin'"pancakes

1 cucumber, cut into very thin strips

6 scallions, thinly sliced

method

Remove the giblets and any excess lumps of fat in
the duck's cavity. Mix the honey and hoisin sauce
together in a bowl, loosening with a splash of warm
water, and then paste all over the duck. Place the duck,
uncovered, in the bottom of the refrigerator (it needs
to dry out) for 4 hours, or overnight. If you have a
cool pantry, that would be perfect.

Preheat the oven to 400°F/200°C and roast the duck
in the preheated oven for 30 minutes. Reduce the
oven temperature to 350°F/180°C and cook for an
additional $1^1/_4$ hours. Check that it doesn't look as if it's
about to burn (it should be dark red-brown but never
black)—if it does, cover it loosely with foil.

When the duck is cooked, either shred the meat with
two forks or carve small slices that each have a little
skin, fat, and meat. Warm the pancakes in a steamer
according to the package instructions.

Serve the duck meat in a warmed bowl, alongside
cucumber strips, scallions, and hoisin sauce. Each
diner takes a pancake, spreads a dab of sauce in
the middle, and adds a few shreds of duck, some
cucumber, and scallion, and wraps it up before eating.

To drink:
Quingdao Chinese beer

㊸ Rillettes

This heavenly pâtélike pork spread is one of French cuisine's best-kept secrets. If you search for rillettes among the treasures of a French charcutier's glass cabinets, you'll probably be sorely disappointed; and if you find it on a restaurant menu, it's probably a fancy, inauthentic version using salmon or goose. But why? The answer is simple: No French cook would dream of spending their jealously guarded cash on something that's so easy and cheap to make at home. And that's the only place you're likely to find the real stuff—sitting proudly on the table of a French home kitchen. So you should either learn some French and start making friends...or, even better, make it yourself. It's absurdly easy, for something that tastes so right.

The word *rillettes* means "planks," which is presumably because the pork falls apart when spread, but retains a rippled texture.

Rillettes are an unsophisticated, rustic creation so don't expect (or try to create) a delicate combination of flavors. The beauty of this dish is its pure, porky simplicity, and the only art involved is in ensuring that your saucepan simmers long and slow. Oh, and some self-control wouldn't go amiss; rillettes improve when left in the refrigerator for a few days.

Rillettes are best served as an appetizer with something tart, such as gherkins, some strong mustard, and a lot of crusty bread.

Rillettes champions
The inhabitants of the Sarthe region in northwestern France (where the legendary Rillettes du Mans come from) eat 26 lb/12.5 kg of rillettes per head each year—100 times more than is consumed in the rest of France.

ingredients

Makes about 3 lb 5 oz/1.5 kg

1 lb 2 oz/500 g pork shoulder

2 lb 4 oz/1 kg pork spareribs, or a fatty pork cut,
such as Boston butt, rindless and boneless

1¼ cups pork fat or lard

2 cups water

1 bouquet garni of 2 sprigs thyme, 2 sprigs
parsley, and 3 bay leaves, tied with string

1 clove

½ tsp allspice

grating of nutmeg

salt and pepper

To serve

gherkins

mustard

crusty bread

method

Cut the meat into 2-inch/5-cm cubes, and chop the fat
into ½-inch/1-cm cubes. Place the meat and fat in a
large, heavy-bottom saucepan with the water, bouquet
garni, and clove. (Don't be tempted to add anymore
water—this method is a sort of gentle steaming. The
pork should collapse, not boil.)

Cover the pan and place it over the lowest heat your
stove can create, using a heat diffuser if you've got
one, or place it in a very low oven, 250°F/120°C. The
pot should just be gently shuddering.

Cook for 4–6 hours, checking and stirring about every
30 minutes to make sure that it's not burning.

Remove from the heat and set aside to cool. Remove
the bouquet garni and clove. While it's still slightly
warm add the spices and seasonings, then take two
forks and gently tear apart the pork, mixing the fat
with the meat. Be careful to keep the "planks" texture
and avoid turning the meat into a paste.

Cover the meat with a piece of wax paper or plastic
wrap and refrigerate for 2–3 days before serving
(although you could eat them straight away). They will
last for at least an additional week in the refrigerator,
but if you put them into sterilized jars and spread a
layer of melted lard on top, they will keep for months.

To serve, drop a spoonful onto a plate beside some
gherkins, mustard, and crusty bread.

**To drink: Some very simple red wine
sloshed into a ballon glass**

44 Osso buco with lemony gremolata

Osso buco translates as "bone hole"—it's basically leg of veal cut into thick steaks and cooked with the bone, packed with marrow, still in. This is one of those luxurious, sumptuous, slow-braised dishes that you can put on to cook and leave for hours. It's even better when cooked beforehand and heated up again for eating a day or two later. Like many braised dishes, it also uses a relatively cheap cut of meat, yet it makes a refined and velvety dish that wouldn't be out of place on a fine restaurant menu.

What makes this dish really sing, however, is the gremolata—a zesty scattering of lemon and parsley that's sprinkled on the meat just before serving. It's as though the osso buco has been patiently sitting there, just waiting for a switch to be flicked, and when the gremolata hits it, an extraordinary range of flavors is turned on.

Oxtail

Many people are put off by the name oxtail, but it is a truly wonderful slow-braised dish a little like osso buco. Although, cut from the tail of a cow, it doesn't taste weird and it is one of those great hidden delights that has been at the heart of British cookery for years.

Veal bones

Osso buco has that delicious unctuousness because the meat is cooked with the bones still in, and as every good chef knows, veal bones are the cook's best friend. They are full of gelatin, which, when slow-braised, is released, creating the extraordinary silky texture of the sauce that goes with the dish. If you can get a bag of thickly sliced veal bones from your butcher, keep them in the freezer for adding to stews, braises, and stocks. Just slip a hunk of bone into the pot to make the sauce thick and deeply flavored. You can also roast the thicker slices of bone for the tender marrow inside them—extraordinarily good spread on sourdough toast.

ingredients

Serves 6 as a main course

$^1/_3$ cup all-purpose flour
8 veal shin slices, about 2 inches/5 cm thick
scant $^1/_2$ cup butter
2 tbsp olive oil
2 onions, finely chopped
4 celery stalks, finely chopped
4 garlic cloves, finely chopped
$1^1/_2$ cups white wine
1 cup chicken stock
salt and pepper
Garlicked Pommes Puree (see page 95) or Risotto
(see page 65—omit the vegetables and add a pinch
of saffron), to serve

Gremolata
finely grated zest of 2 lemons
1 garlic clove, crushed
3 tbsp fresh parsley, finely chopped

method

Mix the flour with a generous amount of salt and pepper, and use it to dust each slice of veal. Take a large, shallow casserole dish with a lid, large enough to hold the meat in a single layer, place it over medium-high heat, and add the butter and olive oil. When sizzling, add the meat and brown it on both sides. Remove and set aside.

Add the vegetables and garlic to the casserole and fry gently for 15–20 minutes, until softened. Pour in the wine, bring to a boil, and reduce by half. Return the browned meat to the casserole and add the stock. Cover and reduce the heat to a gentle simmer. Cook for 2 hours, checking occasionally to make sure it doesn't boil or dry out. Add more stock if it does.

After 2 hours, remove the lid and cook for an additional 30 minutes to reduce the sauce.

Mix the gremolata ingredients together in a bowl.

Carefully lift the veal out of the casserole, making sure you don't lose the marrow from the middle of the bones. Serve on warmed plates with some of the sauce and sprinkle the gremolata over the top. Serve with pommes puree.

To drink: A classic Chianti (Italian red wine)

45 Ceviche of salmon, sea bass & scallops in citrus juice

This is the closest you'll ever get to eating raw sunshine. It's a classic South American dish, and one of my favorite ways to eat good fresh fish—it's a fantastic method for salmon, trout, sea bass, monkfish, tuna, or scallops. A ceviche isn't cooked in the traditional sense, but neither is it raw, because it's marinated in a cocktail of citrus fruit juice. The result is an extraordinarily fresh, zesty, and uplifting dish.

A word of warning: I've tasted many ceviche dishes that have been over-"cooked" because they've been left to stand in their marinade for hours. You may think that longer marinating means deeper flavor, but you really can overcook a ceviche in citrus juice just as easily as under the broiler, leaving you with fish that is dry and squeaky on your teeth. That would be a tragedy, because when this dish is made well, it's sparkling.

Try different flavors

There are a lot of variations on the marinade that work wonderfully—try combinations that include paprika, tomatoes, olives, oregano, or mint. You can even substitute the citrus juices with vinegars, either straight or flavored. Try to match the herbs a little and don't throw too many strong flavors in together, but, most importantly, make sure you have a good acidic base for cooking the fish.

How does citrus juice cook food?

Excellent. I knew I'd be able to squeeze a little food science into this book somewhere. With conventional cooking, when you heat ingredients the protein molecules in them "denature," which means that their structure is loosened and broken down, letting the molecules coagulate, creating the sort of delicious density you see when fish turns opaque and firms up. The heat also kills bacteria. Citric acid has the same denaturing effect on protein molecules, but has less of an effect on the flavor. It also has a preservative effect, creating an astringent environment that either kills bacteria or makes it difficult for them to multiply.

ingredients

Serves 6 as an appetizer

600 g/1 lb 5 oz fish fillets—mix three different types from salmon, sea bass, scallops, trout, monkfish, tuna, lemon sole, or halibut (ask your fish dealer to fillet and skin them, if possible)

zest of 1 lime

juice of 2 limes

juice of 2 lemons

juice of 1 orange

1 fresh red chile, seeded and finely sliced

dash of Tabasco sauce

2 tbsp extra virgin olive oil, plus extra for drizzling

$^1/_2$ tsp sugar

$^1/_2$ shallot or small onion, finely sliced

1 tbsp fresh cilantro, finely chopped

To drink: A gentle, honey-tasting, lightly-oaked Chardonnay

method

Skin the fish, then carefully remove any pin bones that run down the middle. You can use pliers or fish tweezers for this, but take your time because the fish must be bone-free. Cut the fillets into sashimi-thick slices across the grain—about $^1/_4$ inch/$^1/_2$ cm thick.

In a large, nonmetallic bowl mix together all the remaining ingredients, except the cilantro. Place in the refrigerator for about 1 hour—you can leave it for a little longer if you want it a little more "cooked," but no more than 2 hours or it will be overdone. Mix in the cilantro and lay the fish on small plates with a few spoonfuls of the juices. Drizzle with a little olive oil and serve.

46 Whole tandoori chicken

What is a tandoor?

It's a clay oven that works a little like an upright pizza oven—it gets heated to an extremely high temperature and then food is put on skewers, which are placed leaning against the side. The clay itself lends a fair amount of flavor to the dishes cooked and it provides a very even, very high heat. I've used several of these in restaurants in Britain and India, and they are frighteningly hot. Each time I've used one I've managed to burn all the hair off my arm. The chefs told me that this is normal. Perhaps it adds to the flavor? I've also drunk chai (tea) in rural India that's served in tiny clay cups. The cup lends an extraordinary clay flavor to the sweet tea, but what's most surprising is that they are thrown away after use. Good for hygiene, I suppose, but slightly surprising in a place that's extremely poor.

I can understand if it sounds impossible to make a dish this spectacular at home, but stick with me. You really can.

I'll happily admit that this isn't an absolutely authentic dish—for that you would need a tandoor oven (see left)—but even without the tandoor this is still a fantastic meal. The tandoori chicken we know and love refers to deeply flavored chicken that has been marinated in a spice-and-yogurt combination. It needs to be marinated overnight and roasted on high heat—if you have a rotisserie, that would be a perfect way to get the right flavor and texture.

ingredients

Serves 4–5 as a main course

1 chicken, 3 lb 5 oz/1.5 kg
2 tsp garam masala spice mix
1¼ cups plain yogurt
1 onion, finely chopped
2 garlic cloves, crushed
1-inch/2.5-cm piece fresh ginger, peeled and grated
juice of 1 lemon
2 tbsp tomato paste
1 tsp chili powder
1 tsp ground cumin
1 tsp turmeric
1 tbsp paprika (not smoked)
1 tsp salt

To serve

basmati rice, naan, or slipper bread
lime wedges
hot lime pickle

To drink: Kingfisher beer or other Indian beer

method

Cut two slits into each chicken leg and two into each thigh. They should just reach the bone. Make two shallower cuts into the fleshiest part of each breast. These are to let the marinade penetrate into the meat.

Mix all the remaining ingredients together in a food processor and blend to a smooth paste. Place the chicken in a large, nonmetallic dish and cover it in the paste, massaging it deep into the skin and flesh. Place the chicken, uncovered, in the refrigerator to marinate for as long as possible—preferably 24 hours.

Remove the chicken from the refrigerator an hour before cooking to warm it to room temperature. Preheat the oven to 425°F/220°C. Place the chicken in the oven and cook, uncovered, for 20 minutes, then reduce the heat to 350°F/180°C. Baste the chicken and cook for an additional 35 minutes. Turn off the oven and open the door, letting the chicken rest inside for 20 minutes. Serve with rice, lime wedges, and hot lime pickle.

47 Lamb tagine with sticky dates & olives

The word "tagine" refers to both the delicious Moroccan stew and the pot in which it's traditionally cooked, which looks a little like a witch's hat sitting on a plate. Luckily, you don't have to use the traditional pot (a casserole dish with a lid will do), but they are fun and can lend a slight but pleasant clay flavor to the dish.

There are a lot of different recipes for tagine (it just means "stew"), and I've tried hundreds of them since my friends Sam and Kely visited Morocco and brought me back a huge clay tagine pot. They went to so much effort transporting it and keeping it in one piece that I felt I owed it to them to get as much use out of it as possible.

This is definitely my favorite version—I love the combination of the lamb with fruit. The dates break down and turn into a magical sticky goo. A lot of dried fruit can be substituted for the dates—figs are excellent, as are prunes. In desperation I've even thrown in a few handfuls of out-of-date mixed fruit left over from making Christmas mince pies, and it worked wonderfully.

What's with the witch's hat?

The tagine is shaped like a witch's hat for a very good reason: as the stew simmers, the steam condenses on the lid. In a normal pot with a flattish lid, this will eventually condense all over the lid into droplets big enough to fall back into the pot. The same thing happens with the tagine, except they all trickle down the outside of the lid so they drop back into the stew at its edges. This creates a gentle flow of moisture from the edges of the stew to the middle and ensures that the flavors percolate through the whole dish.

Note: Like most stews, this is best cooked the day before eating and reheated.

ingredients

Serves 8 as a main course

3 lb 5 oz–4 lb 8 oz/1.5–2 kg boned lamb
shoulder, trimmed of fat and chopped into
$1^1/_2$-inch/4-cm cubes

4 tbsp olive oil

9 oz/250 g pitted dates

9 oz/250 g pitted olives

3 cups red wine

10 whole garlic cloves, peeled

large handful of fresh cilantro, chopped

couscous mixed with lemon zest and thyme
leaves, to serve

Dry marinade

2 large Spanish onions, grated

4 garlic cloves, crushed

1 red chile, seeded and finely chopped

1 tsp paprika

2 tsp ground cumin

1 tsp ground ginger

1 tsp pepper

To drink:
A spicy Pinot Noir

method

Combine all the dry marinade ingredients in a
casserole dish, add the lamb, and let marinate in the
refrigerator for 4 hours or overnight.

Preheat the oven to 300°F/150°C. Remove the
lamb from the refrigerator. Add all the remaining
ingredients, except the cilantro, to the casserole and
cover. Transfer to the preheated oven and cook for
$2^1/_2$ hours, removing the lid for the last 30 minutes.
Check that the lamb is meltingly tender, stir in the
cilantro, and serve with couscous.

㊽ Paella di Marisco

Paella rules

There are a few rules to making a truly legendary paella:

1. Once the stock is in the pan, shake but don't stir the rice. You want the rice on the bottom to be lightly caramelized (but not burned), and the top lightly glazed.
2. You need a really wide saucepan or skillet, around 12–18 inches/ 30–45 cm in diameter, preferably with a handle at each side. Invest in a paella pan if you can.
3. You will probably need to use several burners on your stove to cook this, so you'll need to turn the pan occasionally to make sure the paella cooks evenly.

I ate my first truly spectacular paella on the hedonistic Balearic island of Ibiza, off the coast of Spain. I had escaped the mayhem and cacophony of the coast and retreated to the dreaming hills for a walk when I stumbled across a trackside restaurant with a broken tractor almost blocking the entrance, and a spicy marital row emanating from within. I popped my head inside, and an old couple paused briefly to say they only served paella, but they had a nice rosado wine if I fancied it. I ordered both.

The paella came still in its pan with the ice-cold rosada alongside. It looked and smelled spectacular, with all kinds of tender shellfish and chicken legs sticking out of it, and the golden rice was a marvel—deep-flavored and light at the top, yet sweetly caramelized and crusty at the bottom. The rice carried the separate flavors of chicken and shellfish, and a scattering of vegetables kept it light. Heaven. Culinary epiphanies always creep up on you when you are least expecting them.

ingredients

Serves 6 as a main course

1/4 cup extra virgin olive oil

2 lb 4 oz/1 kg chicken legs, thighs, and wings trimmed of excess fat

9 oz/250 g squid, cleaned and chopped into bite-size rings

2 large Spanish onions, finely chopped

1 red bell pepper, cored, seeded, and chopped

6 garlic cloves, finely chopped

1³/₄ cups paella rice

large pinch of saffron

3 cups warm chicken stock

1/2 cup white wine

4 large ripe tomatoes, peeled and diced, or 14 oz/400 g canned chopped tomatoes

1/2 tsp hot smoked paprika

1 tbsp fresh thyme leaves

1 tsp salt

9 oz/250 g mussels, cockles or small clams, cleaned

9 oz/250 g large cooked shrimp, shells on

2 cups frozen peas or baby fava beans, thawed

handful chopped parsley

lemon wedges and a green salad, to serve

method

Add a splash of oil to a paella pan and place over high heat. Add the chicken and turn it occasionally until browned but not cooked through, then set aside. Add the squid, quickly fry, and set aside. Reduce the heat to low, add the remaining oil, the onions, and the bell pepper and gently fry for 15–20 minutes, until softened. Add the garlic and fry for an additional 5 minutes. Stir the rice into the mixture and fry for 1 minute. Everything up to this point can be done in advance.

Add the saffron to the warm stock, then add the stock to the rice with the wine, tomatoes, paprika, thyme, cooked chicken, salt, and mussels. Bring to a boil and simmer, uncovered, over low heat for 20 minutes, giving the pan an occasional turn and shake (do not stir) to prevent it from burning on the bottom.

Push the cooked shrimp into the mixture, then scatter the peas, parsley, and cooked squid on top and cook for an additional 10–15 minutes, until the rice is cooked and the stock has almost evaporated. Discard any unopened mussels, cover with foil or a lid, and let rest for 5 minutes before placing the pan on the table with the lemon wedges on top. Serve with a green salad.

To drink: Ice-cold Spanish Rioja rosado (rosé), such as Marques de Caceres

⑭ Jambalaya

This famous Louisiana paella-style rice and meat dish has
two distinct varieties, the Cajun and the Creole. The main
difference is that the Creole type uses tomatoes, and is sometimes
called red jambalaya, whereas the Cajun version is known as brown
jambalaya, the color coming from the browning of the meat.

This recipe is for the Cajun version, and relies on the legendary "Cajun
trinity" of onions, celery, and green bell peppers. This is probably the only
recipe in which you will ever find me recommending that you use green
bell peppers!

The specific ingredients for different versions of jambalaya vary as much as
those for paella, but the Cajun version has traditionally used foods from the
rural swamp areas, such as shrimp, oysters, and alligator, alongside chicken.

Gumbo

What a brilliant name for a dish! This is another Louisiana classic:
a thick soup made with strong stock, meat, or shellfish and that
Cajun "holy trinity" of onions, celery, and green bell peppers. It's
extremely rich, thick, and filling (as you'd expect from a name like
that), and has a deep history combining the cooking and foods
of the French, the Spanish, and the slaves brought from
West Africa. The word "gumbo" originates from the
Angolan word for okra, "kingombo"—okra being one of
the substances used to thicken gumbo.

ingredients

Serves 6 as a main course

2 tbsp vegetable oil

1 lb 2 oz/500 g chicken breasts,
cut into strips

9 oz/250 g chorizo or other spicy sausages

2 onions, chopped

4 garlic cloves, chopped

1 green bell pepper, seeded and chopped

3 celery stalks, chopped

1 scotch bonnet chile, carefully chopped

3 cups chicken stock

$2^1/_2$ cups long-grain rice

1 lb/450 g large cooked shrimp or crayfish

cayenne pepper

salt

method

Heat the oil in large saucepan, then add the chicken and
sausage and brown for 5 minutes over high heat. Reduce the
heat and add the onions, garlic, bell pepper, and celery and
sauté for an additional 10 minutes, until softened. Add the
chile and the stock and stir in the rice. Cover and simmer very
gently for 40 minutes.

Add the shrimp and cook for an additional 5 minutes. Check
the spices and seasoning, adding salt to taste. Serve.

To drink: A smoky Sauvignon blanc, such as Pouilly-Fumé

⑤⓪ Classic German Sauerbraten with red cabbage (Sweet-sour marinated beef)

Time. That's the key to making this classic German feast dish. Three days are required to marinate the beef in a mixture of red wine, peppercorns, juniper berries, and bay leaves in order to develop the full flavor and tenderize the meat, and even the red cabbage takes two hours to cook, so plan ahead, settle in, and have patience. I don't know about you, but when I make a recipe that takes forward planning, such as gravlax, Beef Daube (see page 144), or sauerbraten, I get a tangible feeling of serenity from the imposition of a little structure on my otherwise chaotic life!

ingredients

Serves 8–10 as a substantial main course

4 lb/1.8 kg boneless beef joint
2 tbsp lard or vegetable oil
1 onion, chopped
4 carrots, chopped
2 celery stalks, chopped
2 tbsp all-purpose flour
generous $^1/_3$ cup water
$3^1/_2$ oz/100 g gingersnaps, crumbled
boiled potatoes and Braised Red Cabbage (see opposite), to serve

Marinade

$1^1/_2$ cups red wine
generous 1 cup red wine vinegar
1 cup water
2 onions, quartered
2 tsp black peppercorns, lightly crushed
2 tsp juniper berries, lightly crushed
4 bay leaves
2 cloves
1 tbsp salt
2 tbsp sugar

 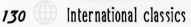

method

Place all the marinade ingredients in a nonmetallic bowl large enough to hold the meat and stir until the sugar and salt dissolve. Add the meat, cover, and place in a cool place for 3 days. Turn the meat in the marinade each morning and evening.

Preheat the oven to 325°F/170°C. Remove the meat from the marinade and pat dry with paper towels. Season with salt and pepper. Strain the marinade and discard the spices and onions. Place a large flameproof casserole dish over a high heat and add the lard. When hot, add the beef and brown it quickly on all sides. Remove it and reserve. Reduce the heat a little, add the vegetables, and fry for 5 minutes. Add the flour, stir, and cook for an additional 2 minutes. Add $2^1/_4$ cups of the marinade and the water.

Cover the casserole tightly, place in the preheated oven, and cook for $2^1/_2$ hours, checking after $1^1/_2$ hours to make sure it isn't drying out. If it is, add more marinade.

Remove the meat from the casserole, cover, and keep warm while you make the sauce. Strain the remaining cooking liquid from the casserole into a saucepan and add the marinade to make it up to about $2^1/_4$ cups. Add the crumbled cookies and simmer for 15 minutes, until it thickens. Season to taste.

Carve the meat and serve with the sauce, boiled potatoes, and braised red cabbage.

To drink: German wheat beer, such as Maisels Dunkel Weisse or Erdinger Weissbier Dunkel

Braised red cabbage with apples

Ingredients

1 red cabbage, quartered, cored, and thinly sliced

$^2/_3$ cup red wine vinegar

3 tbsp sugar

1 tbsp salt

2 baking apples, peeled, cored, and grated

1 onion, finely chopped

$^2/_3$ cup golden raisins, raisins, cranberries, or chopped dates

1 bay leaf

1 tsp cinnamon

salt and pepper

method

Preheat the oven to 325°C/170°C. Mix all the ingredients together in a large casserole dish and season. Cover with a tight-fitting lid, transfer to the preheated oven, and cook for 2 hours, stirring every 30 minutes. Check that it is cooked through and the cabbage is tender. This can be kept in the refrigerator and reheated whenever it's needed.

6. Comfort food

Comfort food

This chapter is dedicated to all the heroic moms, dads, lovers, friends, and carers who cook simple food at home day in, day out, even though they may be tired, grumpy, frustrated or—heaven forbid—unappreciated. It's about food that soothes, and it's the polar opposite of the "Restaurant Dishes" in the previous chapter, or those in the next chapter, "Wild."

I spend my life talking about culinary adventures and championing new or unusual foods in a desperate attempt to make our mealtimes more interesting. I try to inject some fascination into our culinary lives, which seem to get simpler, less healthy, and more monoculinary every year. But I happily put my hands up in the air and admit that everyone needs some stability, comfort, and familiarity to counter the confusion and stress of the modern world. I don't eat golden sausages and palm weevils every day of the week, and, when life gets hairy, I notice that the dishes I cook tend to be the ones in this chapter, my favorite comfort foods.

Comfort food is often about simple flavors, made in a familiar way so that there are no surprises and no revelations. They are about delivering a good, solid carbohydrate hit via smooth, easily munched, easily digested food.

A few of the dishes here may not sound familiar to you—there are French and Italian words here, such as Croque Monsieur and Pappa Pomodoro. But don't fear: These are foreign fripperies used to jazz up the notion of dishes that are absurdly simple, in this case grilled ham and cheese sandwich and thick tomato soup. Naturally, they have the extra something in them that I hope transforms them from everyday foods into something you should eat before you die, but the basic elements are the same. In France, the ultimate comfort food is Cassoulet, and serving this at dinner will probably soften the heart of even the most stony-faced, stick-thin Parisian.

Fish Pie is, for me, the most glorious of all comfort foods: It's so calming, creamy, and cosy that eating it is like being sung a culinary lullaby. Macaroni & Cheese is only a fraction less comforting for me, and Spaghetti Bolognese is wont to get me purring, much to the consternation of my cat Tom, who thinks that purring is very much his job.

This is going to sound a little nauseating, but I have to admit that I prefer comfort food to be the exception to the rule. I tend to use mealtimes to explore and experiment, but that makes the return to these familiar foods all the more wonderful.

I have nothing against simple foods, nor do I have anything against burgers and fries, deep-fried fish, and other fast foods, as long as they aren't eaten every day, at every meal (because that's when people start to get really unhealthy). I count the most overprocessed cheeses in the world as some of my closest friends. Kept as a shield against the slings and arrows of outrageous fortune, comfort food has an essential place in any gastronaut's world.

51 Silky smooth fish pie

Apologies for this, but it's time for a music/food metaphor. Some dishes are like jazz music: Most of the instruments in the band serve as a vehicle to show off the soloist, who dazzles and amuses with virtuosity. Take, for instance, truffle risotto or caviar served with baked potatoes. Other dishes are symphonies, combinations of team-playing instruments that rely on each other to create the overall effect. Most of the dishes in this chapter are symphonic combinations and, as a result, they aren't dramatic or spectacular, but soothing, calming, and heartwarming. I do love grand culinary projects and bold meals that my friends will remember forever, but sometimes the only dish that will do is one that soothes your soul.

Fish pie is the ultimate incarnation of the symphonic dish. The ingredients work together as a beautifully complementary team, creating the physical embodiment of the word "unctuous." It's creamy, slippery, fortifying, healthy, and heavy all at once.

There's nothing complicated here, but I would warn you against overcooking your fish. There's nothing worse than a pie with dry fish that squeaks against your teeth as you eat. And be wary of serving too many side dishes, because all that your guests will really want to go with the fish pie is, well, more fish pie.

The world's largest pie

There are regular attempts at baking the world's largest pie, including a pumpkin pie baked in 2005 in New Bremen, Ohio, that was 2,020 lb/916 kg. Denby Dale in West Yorkshire and East Lancashire in Britain holds regular pie-baking events that result in pies weighing at least 9 tons. The recent millennium pie was 12 tons and 40 feet/12 m long, once listed in the Guinness Book of Records as the biggest pie ever made.

To drink: Sancerre white wine

ingredients

Serves 6–8 as a main course

2 lb 4 oz/1 kg starchy potatoes

³/₄ cup butter, plus extra for greasing

2¹/₄ cups milk

1 lb 5 oz/600 g firm whitefish fillets, such as cod or haddock

14 oz/400 g undyed smoked haddock fillet

3 bay leaves

¹/₃ cup all-purpose flour

handful of fresh parsley, chopped

9 oz/250 g cooked, peeled shrimp

4 hard-cooked eggs, shelled and quartered

4 tbsp melted butter

salt and pepper

minted peas and crusty French baguette, to serve

method

Peel and quarter the potatoes. Bring a large saucepan of lightly salted water to a boil, add the potatoes, and cook for 15–20 minutes, or until tender. Drain, mash thoroughly with half the butter and 2 tablespoons of the milk, then season with salt and pepper, cover, and keep warm.

Place the fish fillets in a shallow saucepan and pour over the remaining milk. Add the bay leaves and place over low heat. Bring the milk to a gentle simmer and poach the fish for 4 minutes (they shouldn't be fully cooked because they will be baked later). Remove from the pan and place on a plate, discard the bay leaves, and reserve the milk. Remove any remaining bones and skin from the fish and flake into large chunks. Put in a bowl, cover, and set aside.

Melt the remaining butter in a saucepan, then stir in the flour to make a roux and cook, stirring occasionally, for 3 minutes. Gradually add the reserved milk, a ladleful at a time, and mix into the roux. Add the parsley, the cooked fish, the shrimp, and the eggs. Fold carefully together. Season with salt and pepper to taste.

Preheat the oven to 400°F/200°C. Butter a pie dish and fill it with the fish mixture. Lay the potatoes on top, making a pattern. Drip the melted butter over the whole pie, place in the oven. and bake for 30–40 minutes, until the top is golden brown.

Serve the pie with minted peas and some crusty French baguette.

(52) Classic French cassoulet

If you've never tasted cassoulet before, you could be forgiven for wondering why the French make such a fuss over a bowl of sausage and beans. It's just cowboy food, isn't it?

Well, yes, if you want to be literal about it, the ingredients include beans, sausage, plus lamb, pork (and often duck), and yet to the French cassoulet is so much more important than the sum of its parts. It's their ultimate comfort food. It's a deeply comforting, maternal dish of soothing creaminess and high nutrition. It's a historical, cultural, and culinary *tour de force*, and what makes it even more exciting is the fact that there are at least three competing recipes, all from southwestern France, each of which claims to be the authentic version. All of them include navy beans (yup, they're the ones used to make our familiar baked beans), but whereas the recipe from Castelnaudry uses pork pieces and pork sausage, the Carcassone version contains mutton and partridge (when it's in season), and the Toulouse version uses Toulouse sausage and sometimes mutton, duck, or goose. To make your life easy, I've merrily cast all of these rules aside and given you a version that is easy to source and make. Heck, if the French can't agree, they surely can't be upset if we cherry pick the best parts!

Cannellini beans

We eat this bean in several forms: The young beans are eaten—pods and all—as dwarf beans, green beans, or snap beans. Flageolet beans are a delicate, prized variety that are semi-mature, usually white or green, and fantastic with lamb. But the most common by far is the large, mature white bean also known as navy bean or pea bean, used in canned baked beans. These are usually bought dried, and are soaked overnight before use.

ingredients

Serves 8 as a substantial main course

1 lb 2 oz/500 g dried navy beans,
soaked overnight

bouquet garni of 4 sprigs parsley, 2 sprigs
thyme, and 4 bay leaves, tied with string

1 celery stalk, roughly chopped

3 onions, 1 quartered, 2 thinly sliced

4 large garlic cloves, 2 whole, 2 chopped

8 cups water

1 lb 2 oz/500 g thick-cut bacon, cut into
large chunks

2 tbsp duck fat or vegetable oil

14 oz/400 g Toulouse sausage or pork sausage

14 oz/400 g lamb shoulder, boned and cut
into 4 large chunks

2 tbsp tomato paste

1 1/4 cups fresh bread crumbs

salt and pepper

fresh green salad, to serve

To drink: A hefty Côteaux de Languedoc red

method

Drain and rinse the beans and put them in a large saucepan with the bouquet garni, celery, onion quarters, whole garlic, and seasoning. Add the water and bring to a boil. Skim off any foam, then reduce the heat to low. Gently simmer for 1 hour, uncovered.

Meanwhile, cut the meat into pieces 1 1/2 inches/4 cm square, then add the duck fat to a large heavy-bottom saucepan and place over high heat. Add the pork belly and brown it all over. Remove and reserve, then repeat with the sausages, then the lamb. Add the sliced onions, chopped garlic, and tomato paste and cook in the remaining fat for 2 minutes. Remove from the heat and let cool.

Preheat the oven to 350°F/180°C. Drain the beans, reserving the liquid but discarding the vegetables. In a large casserole dish, layer beans and meat alternately until they're all used up. Add the fried garlic, onion and tomato paste mixture, and enough of the bean-cooking liquid to almost cover the beans. Sprinkle over the bread crumbs and cook in the oven, covered, for 1 hour. Reduce the oven temperature to 275°F/140°C, remove the cover, and cook for an additional hour.

Check that it's not too dry, adding a little heated bean liquid or water if necessary. Stir the crust into the top of the cassoulet and serve with a green salad.

⑤③ Chicken with 40 garlic cloves

This dish is a refugee from the 1970s that deserves a full-scale rehabilitation into our culinary consciousness. Its name suggests an overbearing, over-enthusiastic use of flavorings, but in fact the longer you cook garlic, the sweeter and more delicate its flavor becomes. It still tastes undeniably of garlic, I admit—hang on, why am I being defensive about this? I love garlic! I'll make a confession: I sometimes cook this with 80 cloves of garlic, and serve the cooked, crushed extra cloves as a paste for dipping the chicken into. But unless you are an alliumaniac like me, that may be going too far.

The beautiful thing about this dish—other than the garlic—is that it's a one-pot dish that takes little effort and can be left to its own devices. This allows you to get down to the task of finding that huge, powerful, tannic wine that never seemed right to drink with the light, refined meals you've been eating.

If there was ever a good reason for buying free-range chickens, it's Chicken with 40 Garlic Cloves. You can really taste the stronger, leaner meat. If I were a chicken, I'd like to end up tasting exactly like this.

The science of garlic

Nutritionists and dieticians of the nonclinical, doubtful-qualification, anecdotal-research variety make claims about the power of many foods—that some are aphrodisiacs, others eradicate toxins, make you happier, sexier, better, strengthen your heart, mind, spleen, or skin tone. I dearly wish that my body and mind could be controlled so easily, but alas, I am generally skeptical about these claims for the simple reason that clinical research rarely finds any of them to be true. Garlic, however, is a different case. There's solid evidence that garlic contains a substance called allicin that, once broken down, has all sorts of antimicrobial effects. On top of that, all kinds of enzymes also present in the garlic work together to produce molecules that offer all types of medical effects: antifungal and antithrombotic (which means that they help to prevent blood clotting, which can help with heart problems). My friend Charlie swears that he has low blood pressure and once had so much garlic that he fainted.

ingredients

Serves 4 as a main course

1 x 3 lb 4 oz–4 lb 8 oz/1.5–2 kg free-range chicken

$^1/_2$ lemon

40 whole, fat garlic cloves, peeled

2 tbsp olive oil

4 sprigs thyme

2 sprigs rosemary

4 sprigs parsley

1 large carrot, roughly chopped

2 celery stalks, roughly chopped

1 onion, roughly chopped

generous 1$^1/_2$ cups white wine

salt and pepper

crusty French bread and a green salad, to serve

method

Preheat the oven to 400°F/200°C. Stuff the chicken with the $^1/_2$ lemon and 4 of the garlic cloves. Rub the chicken with a little oil and some salt and pepper. In a large casserole dish, lay a bed of the remaining garlic cloves, the herbs, carrot, celery, and onion, then place the chicken on top. Pour over the remaining oil and add the wine. Cover with a tight-fitting lid, place in the oven, and cook for 1$^1/_4$ hours.

Remove the chicken from the casserole and check that it's cooked by piercing with a skewer. The juices should run clear. Cover and keep warm. Remove the garlic cloves and reserve.

Place the casserole over low heat and simmer the juices for 5 minutes to make a gravy. Strain, reserving the vegetables.

Carve the chicken and serve it with the vegetables from the casserole. Squeeze the flesh out of the garlic cloves and spread it on the bread, and serve this on the side with a green salad.

To drink: A Pinot Noir from Burgundy, perhaps

(54) Pappa pomodoro
(Italian tomato soup)

Pizza soup experiments

For reasons I can't adequately explain, I have been experimenting for years with instant soupy versions of solid dishes. The instant Greek salad is pretty good—a soup that combines Greek yogurt, olives, and mint. The instant hamburger is a failure—there's nothing nice about liquidizing a bun with ground meat. But Pappa Pomodoro is a pretty nearly perfect version of instant pizza. I was experimenting using chunks of pizza bases, but never quite getting it right—until I discovered that the Italians had been making exactly this for years, using sourdough. I got a little overexcited when I realized this, and tried making quattro formaggio and fish toppings. But the best version really is this Margarita-style soup.

This is a cheap, rustic, but intensely satisfying dish that's essentially a mixture of old bread, a can of tomatoes, and some cheese. It's very cheap to make and it's a whole meal in a bowl. It is also the opposite of refinement—a classically down-to-earth Italian peasant approach to comfort food.

One thing that makes a big difference to this dish is sourdough bread, and I know that not everyone has this lying around the house. Rye bread is a good substitute. You can use ordinary bread, but the sour kick is really good, and without it the dish probably dips out of the top 101 dishes league! My advice would be to buy some sourdough and enjoy it for a few days (it tends to last a lot longer than normal bread).

ingredients

Serves 6 as a simple, filling main
course soup

10$^{1}/_{2}$ oz/300 g sourdough bread
generous $^{1}/_{3}$ cup chicken stock
4 tbsp extra virgin olive oil
3 tbsp fresh sage leaves, shredded
4 garlic cloves, peeled and finely chopped
1 lb 12 oz/800 g canned peeled plum tomatoes
1 tsp sugar
1 cup hot water
$^{1}/_{2}$ cup grated Parmesan cheese
salt and pepper

method

Chop the bread into rough chunks, about 1 inch/
2.5 cm square. Place a heavy-bottom saucepan
over medium heat. Add the stock, oil, and sage and
simmer until reduced by half. Add the bread and
garlic, increase the heat to high, and fry until all the
liquid has been soaked up and the bread begins to
become crispy.

Add the tomatoes and sugar, stir, and simmer for
15 minutes. Add hot water to thin the soup to your
preferred consistency (it should be thick). Simmer for
an additional minute. Taste and adjust the seasoning.

Ladle into bowls, sprinkle a little Parmesan cheese on
top, and serve.

To drink: Peroni beer or San Pellegrino water

55 Beef daube with perfect mashed potato

The name "beef stew" could never do justice to a creation of such perfection as this. Beef daube is a veritable swan of a dish: On the surface, everything that's visible and appreciable is simple, beautiful, and delectable, yet under the surface the reasons for its wondrousness are deep and complex, and bitterly fought over by scientists throughout history to the level of utter unfathomability. The science of braising is one of the most complex culinary processes, involving combinations of reactions and counter-reactions of carbohydrate molecules and amino acids and lord knows how many intermediate structures and unstable phases.

But STOP RIGHT THERE! Luckily, none of this need get between you and the creation of a culinary masterpiece, because you don't need to understand one little bit of the science to cook a masterful daube. You just need to heed my advice and take your time (you have to marinate the beef overnight). Also:

1. Don't use expensive lean meat. You will be wasting your money and it will create a painfully dry stew. You need tough, stringy cuts full of tendons that will turn into unctuous perfection through slow cooking.

2. Brown the meat very quickly without cooking the insides.

3. Start the stew in a cold oven (yes, really) so that the meat warms slowly. Patience is all!

The science of braising

Basically, when we sear or brown a piece of meat before slowly poaching it, we create a type of reaction called the Maillard Reaction, which results in a deliciously heightened meaty, caramelization-type flavor but it does not "seal" a piece of meat. Even though this "sealing" myth was disproved over a century ago, chefs still claim that it happens.

ingredients

Serves 6 as an extremely filling main course

2 lb 4 oz/1 kg shank of beef,
cut into 16 large chunks

1 large carrot, diced

2 large onions, roughly chopped

2 celery stalks, roughly chopped

5 garlic cloves, roughly chopped

bouquet garni of 2 sprigs thyme, 4 bay leaves,
and 2 sprigs parsley, tied with string

3 cups red wine

2 tbsp all-purpose flour

4 tbsp lard or vegetable oil

1 lb 2 oz/500 g carrots and/or parsnips,
cut into chunks

5 cups chicken stock

1 lb 2 oz/500 g mushrooms,
cut into thick chunks

2 lb 4 oz/1 kg peeled potatoes

1 tsp salt

3/4 cup butter

generous 1/3 cup heavy cream

salt and pepper

handful chopped parsley, to garnish

To drink: Château
Musar—a huge red
wine from Lebanon

method

The day before, put the beef, carrot, onions, celery, garlic, bouquet garni, and wine into a bowl and marinate overnight.

Remove the meat from the marinade and pat dry. Strain, reserving the wine, and set aside the vegetables and bouquet garni.

Mix the flour with some salt and pepper in a bowl and toss the beef in it. Add 2 tablespoons of the lard to a large casserole dish and place over high heat. When the fat is smoking, add 2 pieces of the beef and quickly brown on all sides, without letting the meat cook through. Remove and reserve and continue with the rest of the beef. Set aside.

Add the remaining lard to the casserole, add the carrots, and brown them over high heat. Add the browned meat, marinade, stock, bouquet garni, and mushrooms and mix through. Place, uncovered, in a cold oven and heat to 275°F/140°C. Cook for 1 hour, then cover and cook for an additional 2 hours.

Remove the lid from the casserole 45 minutes before the beef is cooked. Bring a large saucepan of lightly salted water to a boil, add the potatoes, and cook for 20 minutes, or until tender. Drain, then pass through a potato ricer with the butter. Add some salt and the cream and mix through.

Lay down a bed of mashed potato on warmed plates, ladle the daube on top, and scatter over a little parsley.

⑤⑥ The ultimate hamburger with thrice-cooked French fries injected with ketchup

This is the only recipe I've ever made that required a hypodermic needle. You can use those "needle-alikes" that you get from the pharmacist for measuring out medicines for kids. They look like needles—but without the needle! This is an exercise in culinary obsession—something that I don't cook very often, but which I save for when I have the time and the inclination to go absolutely nuts with perfectionism. It's fun to do this every now and then, and it certainly intensifies the eating experience, but it does take time, and your friends will almost certainly not appreciate the full extent of your efforts unless you get them involved. I suggest that you invite your best food-obsessed friend over early in the evening, tell him or her

to bring several bottles of wine, and cook your burger and fries over the course of long discussions about the state of the world, love, sex, death, and the relative benefits of the Columbian Exchange.

Why on earth would you cook a French fry three times?

There are very good reasons for doing this. In good restaurants, you'll often find that the best French fries have been cooked at least twice. You need them cooked through so that the middle is fluffy, but you want the outside to be crunchy. Cook at too low a heat and the fries will be soggy. Cook at too high a heat and they will be burned. So the French fries are parboiled to soften them and loosen the exterior for impending fluffiness, then let cool. They are lightly deep-fried at about 250°F/120°C to cook them through to the inside, ensuring optimum fluff-ation, then let cool again. Then they are cooked in hot oil at 350°F/180°C for about 10 minutes, until thoroughly crispy. Drain and season and enjoy.

Injecting with ketchup?

The thing about ketchup is that it's full of sugar, salt, and naturally occurring glutamate. It is delicious, although that's still no excuse for putting it on ice cream, as some of my friends used to do when they were kids (I was probably jealous that my mom wouldn't let me). So if you're going to make the ultimate French fries, you might as well just ketchup them yourself. Just fill the syringe up with ketchup from a bowl, push the stub of it into the middle of the fry and fill it up with as much as you can squeeze in without the fry bursting. Fabulous stuff.

Why is it called a burger?

I always used to think that the "beef hamburger" was a contradiction in carnivorous terms, but it turns out that the original burger was called a "Hamburg steak," originating in the port of Hamburg. It seems that the phrase was first recorded in a Boston newspaper in 1884, although the word "burgher" goes back at least to the sixteenth century, and comes from a modern German or Dutch word meaning "a citizen of a fortified town."

So what is the ultimate burger?

I'd say that the ultimate burger is whichever one is your favorite. But if you think that's a cop-out, I'll just add that if you want to continue with the perfectionism, you should buy sirloin steak, keep some nice clean fat in there, and grind it (not too finely) yourself after chilling it for an hour in the freezer.

To drink: An English bitter such as Old Speckled Hen or Bass

⑤⑦ Perfect macaroni cheese

Of all the soft, soothing, unchallenging foods on the planet, this has to be, well, the softest, most soothing, and least challenging. It was a huge feature of my childhood, alongside its soul sister, cauliflower and cheese. It's safe to say that a large part of me is made of macaroni and cheese.

It's simply a dish of cooked pasta, mixed through with a silky cheese sauce and finished off under the broiler. You can add any type of vegetable to it for a little extra crunch, as in the recipe opposite, but it's still fantastic on its own, and I wouldn't be the tiniest bit offended if you left out the healthy parts.

To drink: White Rioja

Are you a macaroni?
The word "macaroni" has a wonderful variety of meanings. My favorite is as a nickname for a well-traveled young Englishman in the eighteenth century (they were also called "exquisites") who had picked up foreign customs and fashions. It's also a species of crested penguin, and a type of poem combining several different styles. It's also an adjective ("macaronic") to describe any form of verse combining two or more languages. I love language.

ingredients

Serves 4 as a single-course meal

9 oz/250 g dried macaroni pasta

4 tbsp butter, plus extra for cooking
the pasta

$2^1/_2$ cups milk

$^1/_2$ tsp grated nutmeg

scant $^1/_2$ cup all-purpose flour

$^3/_4$ cup grated sharp cheddar cheese

$^3/_4$ cup grated Parmesan cheese

7 oz/200 g baby spinach

salt and pepper

method

Cook the macaroni according to the package instructions. Remove from the heat, drain, add a small pat of butter to keep it soft, return to the saucepan, and cover to keep warm.

Put the milk and nutmeg into a saucepan over low heat and heat until warm, but don't boil. Put the butter into a heavy-bottom saucepan over low heat, melt the butter, add the flour, and stir to make a roux. Cook gently for 2 minutes. Add the milk a little at a time, whisking it into the roux, then cook for 10–15 minutes to make a loose sauce. Add three quarters of the cheddar cheese and Parmesan cheese and stir through until they have melted in, then add the spinach, season with salt and pepper, and remove from the heat.

Preheat the broiler to high. Put the macaroni into a shallow heatproof dish, then pour the sauce over. Scatter the remaining cheese over the top and place the dish under the preheated broiler. Broil until the cheese begins to brown, then serve.

The world's cheapest, greatest micro-recipe

Pasta in garlic and butter is outrageously delicious, and cheap. All you need for each person is 3 oz/85 g pasta, 1 garlic clove, 2 tbsp butter, salt and pepper, and a few gratings of Parmesan cheese. While the pasta is cooking, melt the butter in a saucepan, add the crushed garlic cloves, and fry them gently for about 8 minutes, until they just start to turn light brown. Drain the pasta, add to the garlic and butter, then season and mix through. A scattering of Parmesan cheese and you're done. Simple and delicious!

⑤⑧ Heartwarming chicken soup

In recent years chicken soup has become less of a recipe, and more of a philosophy, mainly because it's one of the all-time ultimate comfort foods. It has traditionally been used as an easy-to-eat-and-digest means of nursing people back to health, and this has given birth to the idea that it's a universal panacea, a cure for all problems and afflictions, psychological or medical.

This is all well and good, but let's get back to the basics here; chicken soup is still a food, and it can be made well or horribly badly. I have eaten a few badly-made chicken soups in my travels across the world, and I assure you that, made badly, it cures no one of anything. The main problem seems to be the use of old chunks of roast chicken to make soup. Now, cold cooked chicken is all very well if you're making a sandwich or a salad, but chicken soup really needs freshly cooked chicken, otherwise the meat will be as tough as old boots.

The second common pitfall is to stint on the broth. To tell the truth, this is more important than the meat, being the vehicle, as it were, whereby flavor is delivered to the senses.

Goldene Yoich—Jewish penicillin

Goldene Yoich means "golden broth." It's so important in Jewish cuisine that it has gained the nickname "Jewish penicillin"—its health benefits were championed as far back as the twelfth century by the rabbi Maimonides. It's often the backbone of Sabbath meals and many say that Friday nights wouldn't be the same without it. The extremely poor Ashkenazi Jews descended from the medieval Jewish communities in the Rhineland would try to get a chicken for the Sabbath and would use every available scrap of it, including the feet, neck, liver, and gizzards. The carcass was then used to make soup.

ingredients

Serves 4 as an appetizer

2 tbsp olive oil

2 celery stalks, chopped

1 large onion, chopped

2 sprigs fresh thyme

4 carrots, diced

2 parsnips, diced

$^1/_2$ large turnip or celeriac,
roughly chopped

$5^1/_2$ cups fresh chicken stock

$10^1/_2$ oz/300 g chicken meat, roughly cubed
(optional)

handful fresh parsley, chopped

2 tbsp lemon juice

salt and pepper

crusty bread and butter, to serve

To drink: A New Zealand
Pinot Gris

method

Pour the olive oil into a large, heavy-bottom saucepan.
Add the celery and onion and gently fry for about
15 minutes, until softened. Add the thyme, carrots,
parsnips, and turnip and cook for an additional
5 minutes. Add the stock and chicken, if using,
and simmer for about 20 minutes. Check that the
vegetables are tender, then add the parsley and lemon
juice, check the seasoning, and serve with crusty
bread and butter.

Chicken stock

You shouldn't throw chicken bones and carcasses
away until you've squeezed, boiled, and crushed every
last sniff of flavor from them. It's ridiculously
easy to do, and you don't need any of the high-
falutin' consommé-fretting fluff that many chefs
advise to make a great stock. Just save all the
bones and parts from your chicken, break them up a
little, and throw them into a large saucepan. Add a
carrot, some celery, onion, and some wine if you have
any, throw in some herbs, such as bay, parsley, and
thyme, then add some salt and a few peppercorns.
Add 8 cups of water per chicken carcass and
simmer, uncovered, for 1 hour. If you don't mind a
slightly cloudier but better tasting stock, crush
the bones with a potato masher, then pass through
a strainer.

(59) Croque monsieur

The ham and cheese sandwich was doing just fine as a classic combination until the French came along and...well...made it better. *Croque monsieur* means "mister crispy." And what did they do to it? They fried it in butter and put the cheese on the outside. Great!

There are now many different versions of the croque—the original from *Larousse Gastronomique* is a straight ham and cheese sandwich fried in clarified butter. It's traditionally made with Gruyère cheese, but you can sometimes buy versions coated in more delicate (but less arresting) béchamel sauce. I was offered one in the Canadian Arctic, which was essentially a ham sandwich floating in a white sauce. I offer you this recipe so that you never make the same mistake.

There's no point wondering what the name means beyond a nickname—believe me, I've explored all avenues and, although there are several stories, I'm not sure that I believe any of them. Suffice to say, the first published occurrence of the name was in Proust's *À la recherche du temps perdu* in 1918, a book more famously known for its mention of little madeleine cakes, which spark a near-transcendental awakening in the book's narrator. You never know, the croque monsieur may do the same for you.

Other variations on the mister crispy are a croque provençal, made with tomatoes, and the croque Norvegien, made with smoked salmon. I wouldn't bother with them; steaming hot tomatoes and bread just don't work, and don't even get me started on broiling smoked salmon!

Croque madame

The French are known for their florid and symbolic naming systems for dishes and cooking styles, but I was less aware of the wit that they used until I saw a "croque madame" on a menu in Paris. This is a croque monsieur served with an egg on top (the masculinity of the dish being effectively trumped, justifiably, by the application of the feminine fried egg). Ha! What I can't quite understand, however, is the fact that in parts of Normandy this is known as a croque-cheval, or "crispy horse."

ingredients

Serves 1 as a quick lunch

2 slices white bread, buttered
2 slices smoked ham
$1/2$ cup grated Gruyère cheese
pat of butter, melted
salt and pepper
mixed greens, to serve

To drink: A crisp
Sauvignon Blanc

method

Preheat the broiler to high. Lay one piece of bread buttered-side up and place the ham on top. Cover with two thirds of the cheese and season. Lay the other slice of bread on top, buttered-side down. Brush the top side with the melted butter and place the bread, buttered-side up, under the broiler.

Broil until browned, then remove. Turn the sandwich over and scatter the remaining cheese on top. Replace under the broiler and cook until the cheese is bubbling and browned. Remove and serve with a salad.

60 Ultimate spaghetti Bolognese

Any food historian or linguist worth their salt will tell you that there is no such thing as a Spaghetti Bolognese. But no one in their right mind would claim that such a thing doesn't exist. So what's going on? Well, the inhabitants of Bologna (the Bolognese) are renowned for their ragùs, meat-based sauces eaten with pasta. In 1982, there was even a recipe issued by the Bolognese chapter of the Accademia Italiana della Cucina, which used beef, pancetta, onions, vegetables, wine, and cream.

But food is like language: It develops, transforms, and adapts to the needs of the people who use it. Although I respect history and the wisdom of the great chefs, I don't think there are unbreakable rules about what you can and can't do with food, and although the linguists would hate it, I love the fact that, in Britain, the name has become corrupted to the wonderful Spag Bol.

So I'd like to throw out all of your preconceptions about Spaghetti Bolognese, and offer you an outrageously twisted version of Spag Bol that discards all the usual rules and makes something that tastes absolutely gorgeous.

What is a ragù?

Generally speaking, a ragù is a meat sauce that's made with a soffrito (a slow-sautéed mixture of chopped onions, garlic, and sometimes other diced vegetables) as its base. It's then simmered with tomatoes, other vegetables, and often wine and herbs to concentrate the flavors.

ingredients

Serves 8 as a main course

4 tbsp olive oil, plus extra to toss
with the pasta

1 lb 2 oz/500 g ground beef

1 lb 2 oz/500 g sausage meat, peeled Italian
sausages, or chopped thick-cut bacon

6 garlic cloves, chopped

generous 1 cup red wine

14 oz/400 g canned chopped plum
tomatoes

1 lb 12 oz/800 g red bell peppers, seeded
and roughly chopped

2 red chiles, chopped

generous $^1/_3$ cup white wine vinegar

small handful of chopped oregano

large handful of chopped parsley

1 lb 12 oz/800 g dried spaghetti

salt and pepper

grated Parmesan cheese and a green salad,
to serve

**To drink: A big hairy
Italian Barolo red wine,
if you can afford it**

method

Heat a wide, heavy-bottom saucepan or casserole dish over
medium heat, add half the oil, and the beef and sausage meat.
Break up with a wooden spoon and fry until it starts to brown,
stirring occasionally. After about 20 minutes add the garlic
and cook for an additional 5 minutes. Spoon off any excess fat
(keep as much as you can bear—that's where the flavor is!)
and add the wine and tomatoes. Stir and reduce the heat to a
very gentle simmer.

Heat the rest of the oil in another wide saucepan, add the bell
peppers and fry, stirring occasionally, for about 20 minutes,
until they start to brown. Add the chiles and vinegar and cook
for an additional 5 minutes.

Add the bell peppers and the oregano to the meat mixture,
and season with salt and pepper to taste. Cover loosely and
let simmer very gently for 30 minutes. If it looks like drying
out, add some more wine. Add the parsley a couple of minutes
before serving.

Cook the pasta according to the package instructions. Drain,
return to the pan, and toss with a little olive oil. Mix the ragù
with the pasta and serve with some grated Parmesan cheese
and a salad.

WARNING
---
this chapter is
NOT for the
FAINT-HEARTED

7. Wild

Wild

What makes this book any different from the hundreds of other books that claim to describe the best foods on the planet? Well, in addition to telling you all about the cosy, yummy, refined dishes on the earth, it tells you about the wild, terrifying, shocking, and life-threatening dishes I think you should try!

I have been lucky enough to visit some strange and wonderful places around the world, and I have come across some extraordinary things that people put in their mouths in the name of flavor, nutrition, and tradition. I've tasted fresh sheep's blood, igunak (rotten walrus), civet cat, and porcupine, and I've turned down dog (on animal welfare grounds) and seal's eyeball (because it was offered to me as a dare).

People often ask "What's the weirdest thing you've ever eaten?" and I have to say, hand on heart and head full of insane culinary memories, that margarine is the weirdest food ever created. It's made using fuller's earth, nickel, caustic soda, and all kinds of bizarre substances that are poured in, centrifuged out, lifted and separated, bleached, and refined. And despite all the high-tech equipment and workers, they still manage to produce margarine more cheaply than a cow squeezing out pure, unadulterated butter.

You see, while the foods in this chapter are wild, extraordinary, and unfamiliar, I hate describing them as weird because they all play a normal, familiar, or sometimes historically important role in the cultures where they originated. One man's weird is another man's snack. The snake skins in the Beijing night market may seem repulsive to us, but they are essential reminders that the Chinese have endured crushing natural disasters, crippling political oppression, and desperate famine and war, and this is the reason why they have a proud history of eating every plant, creature, intestine, skin, and genital that the earth creates. They have had to.

The wild foods here tell us stories about the world around us, but I am not deluded enough to think that you will want to pick up a cane rat at the supermarket or order a plate of yak's penis at your local takeout. You can, indeed, get your hands on a few of these things at restaurants or ethnic grocery stores, and I would encourage you to explore and invent, but all I hope for is to open your mind a little. I firmly believe that with every taste of something that you've never tried before—especially the things that take a little courage and a strong stomach—you become a better person, with a new and extraordinary moment lodged in your memory to toy with, a tale to tell your kids, and a slightly new perspective on life.

These foods may seem gimmicky at first glance, but they tell us an enormous amount about the world, and often about the more difficult and dangerous places in it. I hope that you are an inquisitive soul who likes to travel to understand the world around you and perhaps to empathize a little with the people who live in it. I urge you to try the local foods and to push yourself to share the flavors and tastes of new countries. I guarantee that you'll make a connection, meet new friends, and even, in a brief flash of mutual understanding, go some way toward making the planet a better place.

⑥ Cane rat

Latin name: Thryonomys swinderianus (so much more palatable than the black rat's name, "Rattus rattus"). In Cameroon a decent-sized one will fetch a remarkably high price at market—around $12.

I've tasted some strange and wonderful things in my life: Rotten walrus, fresh goat's blood, several different brands of tear gas, and all kinds of insects. I don't actually go searching for extreme food but rather something revelatory, useful, or world-changing. I'm obsessed with the idea that when Columbus brought the potato back from the New World to Europe, it was treated with great suspicion, much as when I offer lamb's testicle kebabs to my friends. But what if one of these foods that seem weird and unsettling turns out to be the next potato—the next staple food that will sustain millions? That's what I'm searching for.

The nearest I've come to uncovering a revolutionary, potentially world-changing ingredient is this: Cane rat. I'll admit that it didn't look good at first; these little guys are usually caught in the forests of Cameroon, and they are vicious. They have huge incisor teeth built to take your fingers off, they are extremely ratlike, and to cement their place in your nightmares they are the size of a small dog. Added to that, although they aren't endangered themselves, the trade in bush meat (with which they are classed) is severely harming the biodiversity of Central West Africa. Doesn't look good so far, does it?

However, I discovered a farm college in Cameroon that teaches farmers how to domesticate these vicious little beasts, raising them on sugar cane and scraps, and providing a solid income for poor farmers. This protects the wild bush meat, helps alleviate poverty, and encourages sustainability in a fragile environment.

But all of those advantages are wiped away by the greatest revelation of all: Cane rat is DELICIOUS. In fact, I'd say that it's the best white meat I've ever tasted, better than the finest chicken, pork, or alligator meat. It's sweet, succulent, and tender; it's easy to cook, and yields a huge amount of lean meat.

To drink: Cameroonian Guinness (it's sweeter than the usual stuff!)

The only problem is the obvious one: Its name. I can't ever imagine seeing rat in the rodent section of my supermarket, and I don't honestly think the customers in my favorite butcher's would dare to try it. I suggested to the managers of the farm that they could perhaps try renaming it. If they called it the Chicken of Love, perhaps it would fly off the shelves. But this is undeniably a rodent, and it will take a remarkable shift in sentiment for people to take it to heart. It's a tragedy really: My Columbus moment remains at arm's length.

If you do manage to lay your hands on one of these little guys, cut him up into joints, fry him with a little oil, garlic, chile, and tomatoes, then stew him for 30–50 minutes. Serve with manioc (an edible shrub), if you can find some.

⑥2 Sea cucumber

There are only two foods that strike the fear of God into me: licorice (don't know why—just hate the stuff) and sea cucumber (the outrageously palatable name given to what is, unmistakably, to anyone who isn't completely insane, a sea slug).

I usually surprise myself with my enthusiasm for foods that push the boundaries a little, but for some reason sea cucumber is the physical embodiment of all the monsters I ever imagined living under my bed. They terrify me. It's not rational, and I don't know why something so innocuous, passive, and, frankly, defenseless as a sea slug is scary when I'm happy to wolf down jellyfish, cockroaches, and rats, but there it is. Some things can't be explained.

So what, you may wonder, is a slug doing in this book? Well, despite the terror I feel with regard to them, I am also deeply thankful for the experience I had eating one of them and tackling my sluggy demons. On one level I'm a firm believer in the amateur psychology of doing things that terrify you in order to make you stronger. But, more importantly, I love the fact that when I think about the most memorable, extraordinary, and life-defining things I've done, many of them are foods that I've eaten. Fresh goat's blood in Ethiopia, my first haggis in Scotland, and my first Kobe beef in Japan at the age of eight (eating raw meat seemed so naughty).

But the most memorable of all was sea cucumber. In Seoul, the capital of South Korea, there's a fish market where they sell the strangest collection of floaters, clingers, and bottom-feeders I've ever seen assembled in one place. It's like wandering around a natural history museum; the only difference being that here you can buy and eat the exhibits. The sea cucumbers were in huge tanks, separating the spiny ones from the smooth ones, the black from the green. I chose a large spiny blackish-green one (if you're going to confront your demon, he may as well be the largest, scariest-looking one in the tank) and took it to the restaurant level upstairs, where they operate a BYOS (Bring Your Own Slug) policy—bring in the slug and they prepare it for you, charging you a little for the privilege and making their money on the beer, rice, and side dishes they supply alongside.

To drink: Vicious rice liqueurs served in bottles with incomprehensible labels

The chef took my vast, slowly wriggling sea cucumber out of my hands and, without a word, put it on a large log and squeezed down with her hand, whereupon the slug ejected its intestines. "Good, that got rid of them," I thought. Oh how wrong I was. The chef handed the stringy guts to me and told me to eat them straight away "They are the best bit." Ye gods, I was scared of eating the slug itself, let alone its raw, slimy guts! With a shaking hand, I put them in my mouth and chewed. They were a little sour, a little intestinal, and stringy. I chewed, and I swallowed. I stood shivering for a moment, wondering whether I was going to be sick, but I weathered the storm. The chef took a huge cleaver and chopped the (still live) slug into slices and I dipped them, still wriggling, in soy sauce and ate them. They tasted clean and fresh, like squid sashimi, but tough as old boots. It was a horrific and yet oddly cleansing experience. And then a wave of exhilaration swept over me. I had done it! I had confronted my demons.

Now, when I visit places where the food is unfamiliar, ugly, or spiny, I no longer feel trepidation or disgust, because I have been to the culinary depths—I have crossed the culinary Styx—and returned. Still not sure about licorice, mind. That stuff is just wrong.

Sea slug facts

There are 600 different species of these little guys, which survive on nutrients found in seabed sediment. I've eaten them raw, as described above, but also slow-stewed and served in slimy soups. I've never particularly enjoyed the taste and sensation, but I love the frisson! Sea slugs can't swim, but they do have one extraordinary, if rather useless, talent. When scared by predators they can sometimes eviscerate themselves, ejecting their stomach and intestines.

63 Palm weevils

I love trying out new foods, so when I saw palm weevils on a market stall in Yaoundé, the capital of Cameroon, I just had to buy them. They were both appalling and fascinating, each the size of a large thumb, but with a discernible face on them, complete with whiskers. I thought I could make out a wry, knowing smile on their cheeky little faces, but, looking back, I may have been making that part up. As they wriggled orgiastically over each other in a large bowl, I just stared at them with my mouth wide open.

Could these really be edible, or was the enormous market trader selling them as pets, or possibly as vicious guard worms? I asked her, using a complex sign language of hand-to-mouth motions to conquer my inability to speak Cameroonian-inflected French. She gave me a huge beaming smile and said, in plain English, "Oh, yeah, Man, they gooooood!" Ah. And how does one cook them? "Boil them for a few minutes, then grill them over charcoal."

I bought a large bag of the weevils and thanked the market trader, but as I walked away I realized that I had neither a pot to cook them in, nor a charcoal grill to cook them over. I headed for the streetside eating shacks by the central railroad station and went around asking until I found someone who was willing to help me cook them in return for a few thousand francs.

The weevils wriggled ferociously as they were boiled, and then we skewered them on kebab sticks and grilled them over some lovely smoky charcoal and I sat down for lunch.

The weevils still had little black recognizable faces and whiskers, which was nice. I put one in my mouth and bit down. I have to admit to an initial wave of revulsion as the crispy skin gave way to its soft and creamy insides. They tasted a little like shrimp and a little like hazelnuts and were, I was told, packed with protein. The parts I really didn't like were the faces, which cracked as I bit into them. I took to biting the faces off and leaving them on my plate as I tucked in to the fleshy bodies instead.

What is a palm weevil?

The Rhynchophorus phoenicis, or African palm weevil, is harvested from the Raphia palm tree. Although most insect-plant relationships like this are mutually beneficial, with insect activity fertilizing the host plant while the insect takes nutrition from the plant, the palm weevil doesn't. Palm weevils are a true pest, and collecting them and eating them is therefore an excellent idea. The best weevils are about two weeks old. The way to find them is to look for a sick palm that is losing its leaves and turning grayish. The telltale sign is holes burrowed by a caterpillar called Orytces rinoceros, as these and the palm weevils usually attack the same plant simultaneously. They aren't cheap, and will often fetch between 10–50 US cents each in the market. The average monthly income for Cameroonian larvae harvesters is about US$70, which is good for the region.

To drink: Anything you can lay your hands on— usually a strong lager, if you're in Cameroon

64 Deep-fried crickets

Locusts, crickets, and cicadas are all types of grasshopper: insects that have legs specially adapted for jumping. Anyone who's visited Southeast Asia or South America will have been offered cooked versions of these or similar insects at some point, and will have either recoiled at the idea of eating insects or become excited about the possibilities of such an unfamiliar food. I got very excited indeed.

Insects like these are often roasted or, increasingly, deep-fried. Deep-frying is a pretty decent way to cook, as long as the oil has been changed relatively recently. I've tried many types of deep-fried insects and the only ones I didn't like were the ones that tasted of old oil. On the other hand, roasting often doesn't mean the sort of oven-roasting we are familiar with, but is actually dry-frying in a large pan. I've had khi-kheh, Burmese bamboo-dwelling larvae, that were cooked like this, and they were utterly delicious. I swear that they tasted exactly like Jerusalem artichokes—sweet, crunchy, and late developing on the palate, like pistachios.

The first time I saw roasted grasshoppers was in the vast food markets of Bangkok, displayed alongside roasted cockroaches. I ate them both, wolfing down the cockroaches in return for them having kept me up all night in

my hotel the night before. They all pack a decent hit of protein, carbohydrate, and fat for their bulk.

Anyone who doesn't like the idea of eating insects probably doesn't like the thought of eating insect secretions either, but I'll bet they've all tried honey and thought nothing of it. They might also be interested to know that the U.S. Food and Drug Administration sets a maximum limit for insect fragments in flour: 450 per kilogram, so it's probably safe to say that we all eat insects all the time.

But why bother trying to eat insects? They are difficult to catch in any great number and each one provides only a small amount of nutrition. Well, I wonder if there's a connection between crop infestation and insect numbers, and if we start eating those insects, perhaps the crops would do better—you and I could be chipping away at world hunger. One of my favorite food books is *Why Not Eat Insects?* by Vincent M. Holt. It's a little gem that argues exactly this case, although the author has an annoying habit of sounding like he's a bit...well...nuts.

Will insects ever make it as a mass-market food? Well, the prognosis is bleak at the moment, if the reaction of my friends is anything to go by, but I refuse to give up. You can buy crickets and assorted insect mixtures by the can these days, but I admit that it's a fledgling industry. What we really need is a really good Insect Marketing Board.

Other tasty insects to try

I recommend the following: Caterpillars, butterfly larvae, fly eggs (they are tiny), ant eggs (huge and creamy), Mexican wood lice, and, of course, the vast palm weevil [see page 164]. On my wanted list are wasps, cockchafers, and spiders.

To drink: Rough Thai whisky

⑥⑤ Deep-fried scorpions

The Donghuamen night market in China's Beijing is a world-renowned center for weird foods. A long row of stalls lines a street to the east of the Forbidden City (near Wangfujing station) selling silkworm larvae, squab pigeon (eaten whole—wings and all—very nice, too), grilled snake skins, lizards, and grasshoppers. But the weirdest food of all has to be scorpion. I never imagined I'd eat one, let alone a whole kebab of them.

The scorpions are alive, kept in a large steel bucket, and when you ask for a stick of them, the stallholder carefully removes them one by one with a pair of tweezers. They are about 2 inches/5 cm long, measured with their tails curled ready for attack. The stallholder spears them on the wooden stick, while they are still alive, and they wriggle their legs around trying to escape. They don't flail for long though, because the stick is dropped into a pot of boiling oil to cook for about a minute. After that it's drained on paper and handed over for the price of a beer. They are crispy and crunchy, and although it's an odd, scary, and unnatural thing to put in your mouth, they taste of salty potato chips.

The only downside to the night market is that it's touristy—the stallholders beckon you over in broken English, telling bad jokes that they've obviously told a thousand times before, and there's a certain theatricality to the whole affair. But in actual fact the tourists are mainly Chinese, and many of them find the food odd, too, which makes the Westerners wandering the strip feel a lot better.

Even though the Chinese have created a rich food culture based on the principle of eating everything and wasting nothing (see Yak's Penis, page 174), there's been an explosion of fast food culture that would be familiar to anyone in the West. Young people are eating simpler and more mass-produced food than they used to. It's not quite as nutritionally poor as some modern fast foods we are used to, but there's a real sense that young Chinese have much more conservative tastes than their elders. And seeing these youngsters recoil from the more "specialist interest" foods offered is very interesting. It's a little like being at a fair, with young men trying to outdo their friends and impress their girlfriends at the same time, and there's a lot of girly squealing to add to the atmosphere.

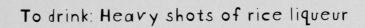
To drink: Heavy shots of rice liqueur

66 Duck feet webs

I never realized that duck feet webs were a viable foodstuff until I visited China. Sure, I've eaten cockscombs (tender like calves' liver, since you ask), chicken feet (you nibble the soft skin off the bones), and chicken gizzards (lean and oddly crunchy), but what can you get out of the skin from duck's feet? Well, a unique experience, if nothing else. They are here in my list of 101 dishes partly because their texture is so extraordinary, but also for the sheer ingenuity of the person who first came up with the idea that you could eat them at all!

As with so many of these foods, the real fun is the texture, and in China duck webs are an expensive delicacy for this very reason, but they are also indicative of an entirely different attitude to food. The Chinese have a strong culture of eating every part of their animals in order to extract every drop of protein. Wealthier nations have become lazy with their food, and it's true that the extremities and innards of animals tend to require more time and technique in their cooking. Many of these ingredients that we now consign to the trash used to be great delicacies in Western countries. Ingredients like spleen, cheeks, genitalia, and duck feet webs take more preparation and often several cooking stages, so our love for them has turned full circle into distaste and even horror.

The webs are rubbery and chewy, and they taste of little other than the fragrant sauces that are served with them. They are a lot of fun to eat, but not when served very cold straight from the refrigerator, when they are even chewier than normal.

Other duck parts

In Beijing supermarkets, you can often find trays of duck heads. Extraordinary things, really. You bite the skin off the heads, which can be cooked in several ways but are often prepared in the Peking Duck (see page 114) style. Then you can eat the tongues and brain, both of which are great delicacies.

Other edible feet

Cow heel pie may be a comic name to you, but cow's feet were often used in the past for stews. Of course, there's almost no meat on a cow's foot, but it is used to add flavor and natural gelatin to a stew. You can buy calves' foot bones from butchers, and if you add one to a stew, it acts as a marvelously unctuous thickener, giving depth and a velvety thickness while avoiding the rapid flavor and clogging texture produced by using flour or cornstarch as a thickener. Chicken's feet are a great delicacy in dim sum restaurants and, again, there's little meat on them: it's the tender skin you're after. Pig's Feet (see page 46) are a great delicacy in many countries and, although not a foot, lamb shank is becoming widely popular again as a slow-braised dish. The reason these are all so popular is that the long, slow cooking they require turns the tendons and skin, which make up so much of the feet, into delicious gelatin.

To drink: Great Wall of China white wine. Warning: It's quite rough

⑥⑦ Caribou

I'm not usually a guilty eater. I've worked out the ins and outs of being a carnivore, and I always try to buy ethically raised, free-range meat, so I feel relatively at peace with eating pretty much anything. But I have a real problem with eating caribou, for one simple reason.

I was once Santa Claus.

It was the winter of 1986, and I was at home from school for the Christmas vacation and broke (as usual), so I took a job at the local shopping mall. I wasn't sure what the job entailed until I arrived and was encased in huge swathes of red polyester and covered in itchy fake wigs and beards. They sat me on a throne surrounded by Christmas trees and fake gifts, shoved a bag of small packages into my hands, and said, "Right, you're Santa Claus." I was 19.

I LOVED being Santa. Who wouldn't? You get to dispense joy, wonder, wisdom, and benevolence to small, bedazzled (and occasionally terrified) children as their adoring parents look on. In many ways, it's a position of ultimate power: Small, sweet, naughty little kids enter the grotto and are instantly transformed by the magic of meeting The Big Beardy Guy Who's In Charge of Gifts into the most well-behaved children on the planet. It doesn't pay to mess with Santa. I only wish that I could wield such mesmerizing power over my own kids these days!

Anyway, my brush with this mythical power has left me feeling a deep affinity with Santa, snow, facial hair, and caribou, because "caribou" are exactly that: Reindeer. And Rudolph is an essential part of the Christmas present equation: no reindeer, no Santa landing on rooftops, ergo, no gifts.

Caribou facts

Caribou are reindeer, but this name is used for wild reindeer in North America. They are Arctic and Subarctic animals that are well adapted to surviving the cold. They eat lichen in winter as well as some leaves and grasses, and they are famous for the vast distances they migrate—farther than any other terrestrial mammal—up to 3,000 miles/5,000 km in a year.

I hoped to avoid ever having to be unfriendly to a reindeer (I didn't want to mess with The Big Beardy Guy In Charge of the Gifts any more than a toddler would), but inevitably, when your job is to travel the world eating food, you end up in sticky situations. I was making a documentary about Inuit food and culture, and was stranded with four Inuit hunters and my cameraman friend Marc deep inside the Arctic Circle. We were 60 miles/100 km away from the nearest civilization (which, incidentally, was the wonderfully-named Canadian town of Igloolik), the ice had closed in around our boat, and our food supplies were pretty low. Luckily, our Inuit friends had brought a bag of meat with them. Unluckily, it was caribou, raw and frozen. I closed my eyes and tried to imagine it was beef, but try as I might, all I could think about was eating Rudolph. It has a rich, slightly gamey taste when eaten raw, but it seemed to have little fat. Oh, forgive me Santa!

It's actually worse than this, because I've now eaten reindeer three times. Once was even in Lapland, to compound my sins. Reindeer stew, it was, and I must admit that I even enjoyed eating it, although there were mitigating circumstances: It was -40°F/-40°C outside, and if I didn't eat it, I might not have made it back home alive.

You can buy caribou jerky in many places—it's made of strips of lean caribou meat that are cured and dried to leave behind a leathery, chewy strip of strong meat. It's similar to South African biltong.

Just one word of warning: The Christmas after I ate the raw caribou, I received a whole pile of tacky gifts. Be careful out there—there's a lot at stake.

**To drink:
Cloudberry beer
and Aalborg Dild
(dill) Aquavit**

⑥⑧ Yak's penis

The Guo-li-zhuang restaurant in Beijing specializes in one very special ingredient: Penis. I am aware that genitalia may not be high up on your current shopping list, but if you ever get the chance, I urge you to try it, for many reasons.

But before I even begin this little journey, let's get the childish stuff out of the way: The world of penis-eating is strewn with double entendre and snigger fodder. When I visited Guo-li-zhuang for a serious TV program about the politics of food, I thought I'd get the laughs out of the way right at the start by saying to the owner, "It's the first time I've had penis in my mouth, but I like it, and I'm going to do more of it." I thought that this would clear the air so that we could talk seriously about the significance of food paranoia and the extraordinary ability of the Chinese to extract every ounce of protein from their food sources. Oh, how wrong I was. Both my translator and my Chinese Communist Party minder were female, and giggled maniacally throughout the entire penis feast, despite the female manager looking over her spectacles at them like an unimpressed school principal. Oh well.

There is, however, a great deal of cultural and historical importance attached to eating penis in China. The country has had a long history of famine and war (much of it in living memory), as well as its fair share of natural disasters, and this has led to a heightened awareness and ability to extract as much nutrition as possible from all foodstuffs. Feet, skins, spleens, bladders, and heads are all used in Chinese cooking, and why not? While many of us have become conditioned to think that anything unfamiliar is "yuck," a lot of the parts we throw away end up in our food anyway, albeit crushed up into sausages and burgers. In a world where food supply is looking more precarious and expensive every day, we would do well to make use of every morsel available, and eating yak's penis is a wonderful symbol of this.

Genitalia are actually a delicacy in China, and the patrons of Guo-li-zhuang (other than my companions) were exclusively male. There appears to be another reason they enjoyed eating penis: It's a renowned aphrodisiac, giving the consumer heightened sexual performance as well as attractiveness. Apparently. I can't vouch for that, because sadly I wasn't in the company of my wife on my visit, but our driver, who ate his fair share of the genital feast, certainly had a huge grin on his face the next day.

So what does yak's penis taste like? Well, it's hard to describe. Penile, really. It's a relatively clean tasting and unfatty meat, so it takes the flavor of the fragrant broth that it's poached in, but the texture is all: It's chewy—almost bouncy—on the tooth, and there's an undeniable crunch when your teeth cut through it. The sensation is extraordinary and hard to explain because, basically, it feels and tastes like you're eating a penis.

How to cook a yak's penis

Should you find yourself with a 12-inch/30-cm yak's penis knocking around your refrigerator but not a clue how to cook it, fear not. I will tell you all you need to know:

Blanch the penis in boiling water for 30 seconds. Skin it, then cut it in half lengthwise using a pair of poultry scissors. Lay each half flat on a cutting board and, using a knife, make little nicks all along one side of the penis at 1/4-inch/5-mm intervals. Cut the penis into 2-inch/5-cm sections. Make a broth of vegetable stock flavored with lemon grass, cilantro, chile, and toasted sesame oil and bring to a boil. Drop the penis chunks in for about 1 minute each. They will curl up into incongruously pretty penis flowers. Serve with soy sauce for dipping.

To drink: Deer penis juice (a deer penis is left in a bottle of pure alcohol for a year, then drunk)—ouch

⑥⑨ Camel's hump

I milked my first camel in the Middle East. She wasn't enormously eager to begin with (in fact she nearly booted me across the Negev Desert), but she eventually came around to the idea and delivered me a handsome draught of fine, thick milk that tasted surprisingly uncamel-ey, but rather clean and clear, like fresh pasteurized cow's milk.

She was large and cantankerous, but so important to Bedouin culture that she cost far more than the small, cantankerous, yet infinitely more useful automobile that my Bedouin friends drove me around in. The camel has enormous symbolic value to many Arabs, yet it's also an important source of food across North and Central Africa and the Middle East, and was written about as a banquet food by the ancient Greeks, who told of it being roasted and presented whole.

Camels are vast creatures, providing several hundred pounds of meat each. The ribs are highly valued, as are the loin and breast, but the most valuable and prized cut is without question the hump. It is often served slow-braised and then battered and deep-fried, and this is the way I have eaten it. The taste is intriguing: it's halfway between the delectably succulent haute cuisine of Kobe beef (see page 72) and the baldly fatty junk food hit of processed meat. It's soft and tender and, like its milk, it's very uncamel-ey. I can't tell whether its one of the finest things I've ever eaten, or one of the worst, and I've included it in my 101 dishes in the hope that one day you will try it, too, and help me decide!

What's inside a camel's hump?

At school I was taught that camel's humps are used for storing water, but annoyingly, this isn't true. In fact humps are made mostly of fat and are used as energy reserves, a little like the hump of fat that sits above the rump of the fat-tailed sheep. The camel can absorb the fat and flesh as nutrition as food supplies run out. The hump has the additional function of insulating some of the camel's vital organs from the effects of solar radiation—there's little blood flow in the fat and it is a poor conductor of heat, making it instead a good insulator against the beating sun. In fact, the camel's extraordinary ability to survive for such long periods without drinking comes partly from the fact that when they do drink, they drink a huge amount.

Camel facts

Camels can live for between 60 and 80 years. The single-humped dromedary is by far the most common, outnumbering the double-humped Bactrian camel by about 10 to 1.

Llamas and alpacas also belong to the camelidae family, and are know as cemelids. They are able to withstand extremes of body temperature and water content that would kill many other creatures, and they only sweat when their body temperature rises above $106°F/41°C$, unlike myself, who sweats whenever the temperature exceeds $71°F/22°C$. They have extraordinarily long, flirty eyelashes but, despite that, they are the grumpiest animals I have ever met. I rather respect them for it.

To drink: Camel's milk, if you can find some

Thousand-year-old eggs are not, strictly speaking, a thousand years old, although they certainly taste as if they are. They are actually duck or chicken eggs that have been salted in a heavy brine with tea leaves, lime, and lye, then preserved in clay, lime, salt, and ash for anything from a few weeks to several months.

⑦⓪ 1,000-year-old egg

When you open a 1,000-year-old egg, the first thing that hits you is an extraordinary sulfurous smell, which may induce nausea or delight, depending on your palate. The second thing you notice is the extraordinary color; different methods produce different results, but often the egg white changes to a dark-brown, caramel-like gel, while the yolk has turned dark blue-green or black. Sliced open it looks extraordinary; although every synapse of your brain will be working overtime to inform you that you should not, under any circumstances, eat it.

I think that you should ignore the natural revulsion to this egg, overcome your fears and try eating 1,000-year-old eggs, not just for the adventure of the experience, but because they will take you on a vivid historical journey. This is an ancient method of preserving excess eggs for times of need, and the taste and texture is exactly the same as that experienced by people in the Ming Dynasty 500 years ago. Now that's what I call living history!

You can buy these eggs from most Chinese supermarkets, but while I am a fervent advocate of them, I'd suggest you don't buy too many—a little goes one heck of a long way.

To drink: Chinese rice wine

Don't make your own 1,000-year-old eggs

This is the simple method of making 1,000-year-old eggs—this is for information only, and you shouldn't under any circumstances try this yourself. The eggs are first soaked in a heavy brine mixed with lye for two weeks, then a strong tea infusion is made and mixed with a lot of salt, quicklime, and wood ash. This paste is highly corrosive, and should not under any circumstances be touched with bare skin. The eggs are covered in the paste and left for about three months before they are ready to eat.

1,000-year-old egg recipes

You can slice these through the middle to display their beautiful concentric rings and serve them as they are, but there are a few recipes for them, too. You can chop them up and add them to omelets, wrap them in pickled ginger, or slice them over tofu topped with ginger and scallions. Another famous serving method is to chop them with pork and rice porridge to create an extraordinary congee, although I think you need to have a pretty tough constitution to stomach that unless you've grown up in or near China.

8. From
the sea

From the Sea

I always chuckle when I look at my fish cookbooks. They usually seem to be struggling for their identities, because a huge portion of each book is taken up with an encyclopedic list of information, with descriptions and diagrams, information on the different species, where they come from, and whether they are pelagic, scaly, fresh- or salt-water dwellers. It's all interesting stuff, but they often have very few recipes, for one good reason: The best way to do justice to almost any really good, really fresh fish is to slip it under a grill and then eat it quick.

Okay, I know that there are a good few things to do to a fish given the will and the means, but I've tasted so many overcomplicated and over-tickled fish dishes, where I wish the chef had just stopped messing around and saved a noble creature from a gastronomically confusing end. One of the great fishy travesties has to be the bizarrely popular filets de soles mornay—sole fillets drowning in a cheesy béchamel sauce—a culinary crime that the French routinely commit, sapping the life and flavor out of a fine, delicate, and expensive fish. I always wonder how such a cultured, gastronomically aware nation can get something so wrong.

Luckily, I don't need to fill 250 pages with fish-related material, so although the sardines and whole roasted tilapia recipes are pretty straight "apply strong heat to fish" dishes, the rest of my favorite dishes still explore a little with the ingredients and the methods. The key, however, is still simplicity. Linguine with Clams is my wife's favorite way to eat both pasta and shellfish, and it's more about assembly than cooking. Easy, Finger-Licking Garlicky Shrimp is one of the simplest recipes in the world, yet it has such an intensity of flavor that it yells its glorious flavors across your palate.

I have, as a little test of your adventurousness, given a couple of longer recipes for Bouillabaisse and Crab Soufflé, but they are all about getting maximum enjoyment out of the main ingredients, and not about creating something newfangled. Indeed, Bouillabaisse is as old as the hills.

A little word about sourcing your fish, if I may be so bold. I know that budgets are tight and old habits are hard to change, especially when families need to be fed and difficult food paranoias need to be accommodated, but choosing your fish could go a long way to changing the world for the better. If you can afford it, try to avoid fish whose stocks are endangered or whose farming is ecologically destructive. Try to buy wild, rather than farmed fish, line-caught and handpicked rather than trawled, and watch out for jumbo shrimp, often from Southeast Asia, that have been farmed in ways that destroy local communities.

If we give the producers and fishermen an incentive to look after them, we may be able to sustain their stocks for generations to come, and thereby enjoy eating fish for ever!

⑦ Linguini with clams

This is my wife's favorite pasta dish, and for good reason. It looks great, it tastes great, and there's even a little element of engaging with the food itself by getting your fingers messy. I like that. I just wish it was a little more difficult to make—whenever I cook this I feel as though I've left some important stage out because it's just so outrageously easy.

Like many of the great recipes in this book, this is an old classic involving no invention or creativity on my part. It's just a combination of shellfish flavored with a little garlic, olive oil, and parsley. It's pure and simple, but it sings in your mouth.

The only note of caution here is to make sure your clams are clean—there's nothing sexy about a mouth full of sand and grit. Make sure you use thin pasta, otherwise the clams can get lost in the mêlée.

You can use this recipe for all kinds of shellfish—if you're in France, you might be able to find little "tellines," the small triangular clams that don't offer a huge amount of meat, but taste outrageously sweet and look great. Cockles make a wonderful and cheap alternative, too.

The one-minute pasta course

Pasta shapes can be confusing. Why should you use farfalle instead of spaghetti or penne instead of orechiette? It's all a matter of matching the pasta to the sauce. Generally speaking, the finer sauces call for a thinner pasta, whereas the chunkier ragùs and thick creamier sauces call for a wider one. You'd use a large blankety flat one like pappardelle to carry a nice thick, chunky wild boar sauce, but a thinner spaghetti with a fine Bolognese-type sauce. Chunks of salmon might match penne in size, so they don't all slide to the bottom of the bowl, and orechiette seem to work beautifully with little broccoli florets and good pesto (then again, anything works with a good pesto). The main thing to remember is not to add too much sauce—you should be able to taste the pasta and feel its texture in your mouth. The sauce should coat the pasta, rather than smother it.

ingredients

Serves 4 as an appetizer

7 oz/200 g dried linguini pasta

3 tbsp extra virgin olive oil

4 garlic cloves, finely chopped

2 shallots, finely chopped

$1/2$ fresh red chile, finely chopped

$1/2$ cup white wine

2 lb 4 oz/1 kg fresh clams, cleaned

handful of parsley, chopped

zest of 1 lemon

salt and pepper

method

Cook the linguini according to the package instructions, drain, and toss with a splash of olive oil. Cover and keep warm.

Add half the olive oil to a large saucepan with a lid and place over high heat. Add the garlic, shallots, and chile and cook gently for 8–10 minutes, until softened. Add the wine, bring to a boil, and cook for 2 minutes. Add the clams, cover, and cook for an additional 2–5 minutes, or until all the clams have opened—discard any that haven't. Add the drained linguini, parsley, lemon zest, the remaining olive oil, and some salt and pepper and mix through.

Serve in warmed bowls, with another bowl for discarded shells.

To drink: A mellow, oaky Chardonnay

⑦2 Thai salmon laksa

Something magical happens when you combine the classic gang of Thai flavors: cilantro, ginger, lime juice, toasted sesame oil, red chile, fish sauce, and coconut milk. On their own they are great ingredients, but when they are mixed together it's alchemy, producing a sauce that's fresh and uplifting, strong yet delicate, velvety yet zesty. It's my favorite set of flavors, which is one of the reasons I love exploring Thailand. There's nothing better than eating a bowl of grilled fish and noodles spiced with this sauce while sitting in one of those fantastic shack restaurants on a beautiful Thai beach, cooled by a sea breeze.

My Thai friend Pla says that salmon is actually pretty rare back home but she agrees that it's a wonderful way to eat a laksa. And she should know because her name, Pla, means "fish." Laksa is a name for noodle (it's derived from the word meaning "slippery") and this is a classic noodle soup. It's a big and very filling dish, so you don't need huge bowls of it.

ingredients

Serves 6 as a substantial main course

juice and zest of 2 limes

2 tbsp sunflower oil

1 red chile, seeded and finely chopped

4 garlic cloves, peeled and crushed

1-inch/2.5-cm piece fresh ginger, peeled and grated

1 tsp ground coriander

small bunch of fresh cilantro

1 tbsp sesame oil

3 tbsp nam pla

2¼ cups vegetable stock or fish stock

3¼ cups canned coconut milk

3 carrots, peeled and very thinly sliced

14 oz/400 g noodles

1 tbsp sesame oil

1 tbsp vegetable oil

½ cup broccoli florets

1 lb 2 oz/500 g salmon fillet, skinned, boned, and cut into slices half the width of a finger

1 tbsp chopped cilantro leaves, to garnish

Super-quick cheat's laksa

You can find green curry paste everywhere these days, and it's wonderful stuff. For a version of this dish that's really quick to prepare, yet still tastes great, put a spoonful of curry sauce into a saucepan with a can of coconut milk and bring to a gentle boil. Throw in a few thinly sliced vegetables and some noodles and simmer for 4 minutes. Turn off the heat, drop in some salmon chunks, and let sit for 3 minutes before serving.

method

Put the first 9 ingredients in a food processor and blend to a paste.

Place a large saucepan over medium heat and add the paste. Fry for 1 minute, then add the stock, coconut milk, and carrots and bring to a boil. Simmer gently for 10 minutes while you cook the noodles according to the package instructions. Drain the noodles and return to the warm pan with a splash of sesame oil and vegetable oil. Cover.

Add the broccoli to the liquid, bring back to a boil, and then turn off the heat and add the salmon slices, gently stirring them in. Let stand for 3 minutes.

To serve, place a handful of noodles in each bowl, then ladle in the laksa and sprinkle some cilantro leaves on top.

To drink: Singha beer from Thailand

Kho Nang Yuan

This is an absurdly beautiful trio of tiny islands bound together by one sandy beach. It's almost a parody of a tropical paradise island, with a small restaurant and loads of little huts that you can stay in. The food is wonderful, if a little more expensive than in the restaurants across the water on the main island, but then they have to ship everything over in boats, including all the water for drinking, cooking, and washing. One evening when I was staying there, the combination of a fantastic Thai laksa and the ridiculously wonderful setting threw me into such an ecstatic daze that I asked my way-out-of-my-league-beautiful girlfriend a crazy question I never thought I'd ask. We are now happily married with two sweet, naughty little girls.

⑦ Mussel & chorizo stew

This is intense and powerful food that mixes sweet, tender shellfish with strong, spicy Spanish sausage to create a dish that's bursting with flavor. It reminds me of everything that's good about Portuguese cuisine and, to cap it all, it's quick and cheap to make. You don't need a huge amount of it because the ingredients produce a deliciously fragrant sauce that is perfect for mopping up with some crusty bread.

The classic version of this is made with clams, but I think that the strength of the chorizo sausage blows away their delicacy, so I prefer it with mussels. The best thing to use with this is uncooked chorizo, but if you can lay your hands only on the cured stuff, that's fine, too. If you can find a jar of little sweet piquillo peppers, too, all the better.

To drink: A good red Rioja

Instant garlic oil

This is a ridiculously good accompaniment to the dish. Peel and halve a garlic clove, then crush it ruthlessly against the plate, using either your palm or a rolling pin until it squashes and its juices ooze out. Set it in the middle of the plate and pour a little lake of fine extra virgin olive oil on top of it, creating a delicious, rustic oil for dipping bread into. Your guests will love it, and you'll be adding more oil to the bowl before you know it. In southern France and northern Spain, you can buy little saucers with a roughly scored center, which are especially made for this—you grate the garlic in the middle and pour the oil on top. I can't stop buying them.

ingredients

Serves 4 as a main course

2 lb 4 oz/1 kg mussels

2 tbsp olive oil

1 lb 2 oz/500 g chorizo sausage (preferably raw), chopped into $1/2$-inch/1-cm slices

9 oz/250 g bacon (in one piece if possible), roughly chopped

3 large garlic cloves, chopped

4 tbsp butter

$1/2$ teaspoon hot smoked paprika

1 small jar sweet piquillo peppers, drained, or 1 large red bell pepper, roughly chopped

$2/3$ cup white wine

generous 1 cup chicken stock

large handful of parsley, finely chopped

crusty fresh bread, to serve

Variations

Try using Palourdes clams if you're feeling rich, cockles if you're feeling poor. Razor clams are fun and spectacular, and the whole thing takes on a different dimension if you add some saffron threads, soaked in a little warm water, at the same time as the mussels.

method

Clean and debeard the mussels, discarding any that don't close when tapped, or that are broken.

Place a large casserole dish over high heat and add the olive oil. When hot, add the chorizo and bacon and fry for about 10 minutes, until they just start to brown. Reduce the heat, add the garlic, butter, paprika, and piquillo peppers, and fry for an additional 2–3 minutes, until softened.

Add the mussels, wine, and stock, increase the heat to high, and put the lid on. The mussels will start to open as soon as the stew starts to bubble. They need to cook for about 1 minute after they have all opened. Discard any that remain closed.

Ladle into large bowls with the juices, scatter over some parsley, and serve with some good, fresh bread.

⑦⑷ Sea urchin roe

Sea urchins don't look particularly edible, it's true, but cut open one of these little guys and you're in for a rare and wonderful treat. Inside that hard, prickly shell lies a cache of delicious, extraordinarily sweet meat. It's eaten raw straight from the shell (using a teaspoon to dig it out) and it's highly prized by those in the know, especially around the Mediterranean.

If you've ever trodden on one of these while swimming, now's the time to get your own back; a sense of revenge does wonders to heighten the perception of taste! Sea urchins have spiny shells that protect them extremely well from most predators, but they didn't bargain on meeting you wielding a trusty pair of kitchen scissors and a sense of righteous anger, did they? Hah!

The tricky part is in getting your scissors through the shell to begin with. I'd recommend using a pair of rubber gloves, or if you have found some particularly spiny critters, a pair of gardening gloves. Jab the scissors into the urchin and then cut around. Try to keep the urchin flat while you do this because it will probably have some sea-water-cum-juice inside, which is delicious to sip alongside. There's no neat way of doing this, so don't worry that you've made a bit of a mess.

The part that you eat is the roe, or coral, inside the urchin. It's usually in five little orange clusters and the idea is to dig them out with your spoon. There's not a lot of meat on these little things, but it's a very rich flavor. It's not even really an appetizer-size dish, but rather it's a taste or a sensation to get your appetite going. You can drip a little lemon onto the roes, but I prefer to eat them clean and serene.

Bottom-feeders

Sea urchins are relatively common in the Mediterranean and its markets. In France, they are called oursin and wherever you find them, you're also likely to come across another peculiar delicacy called violets. These are usually muddy, crusty-looking fist-sized clumps that break open to reveal a yellow meat similar to akee or scrambled eggs. They are a fun, but acquired taste.

To drink: Chablis
premier cru

⑦⑤ Bouillabaisse

This is a legendary Mediterranean fish stew from Marseilles in the south of France. The taste of this dish is a near-perfect distillation of all the flavors of a summer vacation spent near the sea—the fresh fish, delicate tomatoes, finest olive oil, exquisite seawater broth, and the finest saffron, best eaten outdoors in the brightest sunshine with a large, super-chilled glass of rosé wine.

The genius of bouillabaisse is in the different textures of fish that are used. Some are good, firm heavy hitters that are eaten in chunks, and some are smaller, delicate fish that disintegrate in the cooking process and make up the sauce in which they're poached. There's also a very specific technique to making bouillabaisse, and it's all about boiling the stew in the later stages. This is supposed to help to emulsify (combine) the oil and water or wine in a magical suspension that makes the dish taste so good.

So, although I'm not usually fond of recipes that need strict interpretations and an ingredients list that's set in stone, I have to admit that this one is a little different. I'd go as far as to say: Don't make this dish unless you can find the right fish, otherwise you'll wonder what on earth I was making such a fuss about.

ingredients

Serves 8 as a main course

2 lb 4 oz/1 kg selection of at least 4 different firm white fish fillets, such as red snapper, sea bass, eel, or monkfish, scaled and cleaned, but not skinned

generous ¹/₃ cup olive oil

2 onions, finely chopped

1 fennel bulb, finely chopped

4 garlic cloves, crushed

2 lb 6 oz/1.2 kg canned chopped plum tomatoes

6 cups fish stock

pinch of saffron strands

grated zest of 1 orange

bouquet garni of 2 sprigs thyme, 2 sprigs parsley, and 2 bay leaves, tied together with string

1 lb 2 oz/500 g mussels, cleaned

1 lb 2 oz/500 g cooked shrimp, shell on

salt and pepper

crusty French baguette and Rouille (see page 101), to serve

To drink: A strong rosé from the Languedoc

method

Carefully pin bone the fish, then cut the fillets into bite-size pieces.

Heat the olive oil in a very large skillet or wide saucepan with a lid and gently fry the onion and fennel for about 15 minutes, until softened. Add the garlic and fry for 2 minutes, then add the tomatoes and simmer for 2 minutes. Add the stock, saffron, orange zest, and bouquet garni and bring to a boil. Simmer, uncovered, for 15 minutes.

Add the fish pieces, mussels, and shrimp and cover the skillet. Simmer for an additional 5–10 minutes, until the mussels have opened. Discard any that remain closed. Check the seasoning.

Serve with some crusty baguette and rouille.

⑦⑥ Crab soufflé

Soufflé is one of the great culinary gifts that the French have given the world, alongside Poilane bread, crème brûlée, the croissant, and Juliette Binoche (okay, she's not strictly speaking a culinary gift, but hey).

The master of the soufflé was the nineteenth-century celebrity chef Antonin Carème, who was obsessed with them. The word itself means "breathed" or "puffed up," and the mark of a great soufflé is an ethereal lightness balanced by a delicate flavor. Crab is a fantastic way to eat soufflé, and although many people are scared of making food like this for the first time, due to the popular perception that the collapsed soufflé is the definition of culinary disaster, it's actually pretty easy as long as you abide by the simple rule of NOT OPENING THE OVEN DOOR!

The problem with soufflés is that the complex process whereby the mixture rises once it's baking can be catastrophically disrupted by any changes in temperature, which is why NOT OPENING THE OVEN DOOR is essential.

The base ingredients are a roux of cooked flour and butter mixed with egg yolks and the pre-cooked crab. It's simple, really, as long as you remain calm, follow the cooking method closely, and remember the rule about NOT OPENING THE OVEN DOOR.

Crab evolution

I've always thought that crabs (and lobsters) look somehow prehistoric. It's that exoskeleton thing. Well, funnily enough, I recently discovered that they are, because the first crabs evolved in the Jurassic period. There are around 4,500 species of crab, including varieties that swim, and others that can grow to a terrifying 12 feet/3.6 m across.

ingredients

Serves 4 as a main course

1 clove

2 small shallots, peeled, 1 finely chopped

generous 1 cup milk

6 black peppercorns

1 bay leaf

2 tbsp butter, plus extra for greasing

scant $1/4$ cup all-purpose flour,
plus extra for dusting

4 eggs, whites and yolks separated into
separate bowls

$1/2$ tsp cayenne pepper

9 oz/250 g cooked crabmeat

green salad and crusty bread, to serve

Scary crabs

My scariest crab experience was on the idyllic Thai island of Koh Nang Yuan when I went for a walk up a perfect little hill. It was infested with land crabs, which made a cacophonous clatter scuttling around in a panic as we approached. It just seemed so wrong to meet thousands of these disconcertingly large, land-based crabs, scrabbling about on the ground and even climbing trees. We had a fleeting glimpse of the view from the top, then ran back down before the crabs had a chance to tear us limb from limb.

method

Preheat the oven to 400°F/200°C.

Push the clove into the whole shallot and place in a small saucepan with the milk, peppercorns, and bay leaf. Heat until just simmering, then remove from the heat and let cool. Strain, reserving the milk and discarding the solids.

Carefully grease a 4-cup, high-sided soufflé dish, then dust with flour, tipping the dish around so that it is completely coated. Discard any excess.

Place a saucepan over low heat and add the butter and the chopped shallot. Cook for about 5 minutes, until the shallot is softened. Add the flour and cook for 3 minutes, stirring, to make a roux. Remove from the heat and add the milk a little at a time, stirring continuously so that it doesn't become lumpy. Add the egg yolks and cayenne pepper and beat them in thoroughly with a whisk. Add the crabmeat and warm through again, but don't boil. Pour into a mixing bowl.

In a separate bowl, whisk the egg whites until soft peaks form. Add to the crab mixture one quarter at a time, very gently folding through. Spoon into the soufflé dish, place in the preheated oven, and bake for 25–30 minutes, until golden on top. Do not open the oven door until it's cooked.

Spoon onto plates and serve with a green salad and crusty bread.

To drink: A dry Riesling

⑦ Easy, finger-licking garlicky shrimp

Some recipes are too good and too simple to change, and this is one of those. In the past, I've tried new ways of cooking shrimp using complex haute cuisine recipes, but every time I stray from my old faithful recipe, I return to it convinced that there is no better way to enjoy them than this absurdly simple and crushingly delicious dish.

My method of serving these shrimp is simple: Put the cooked shrimp into a large bowl and place it in the middle of the table. Put a pile of bread next to it with some butter. Give each person a plate, a knife, and a napkin. Then dive your hands into the bowl of shrimp and before anyone can get a grip on what's happening, start eating them as fast as you can! You can, of course, place a few on each person's plate, but I really think that's a little over-the-top when this is such a simple dish.

The bigger the shrimp you buy, the more meat there will be per pound, but the less fun there will be getting at it. Incidentally, I like the shrimp that have little pink eggs underneath them—I chew them off as if they are caviar, and if the shrimp are tender enough, I'll eat the smaller legs, too. You, of course, may do as you please, but I'd encourage you to try a nibble. And if you have enough shells left at the end of lunch, you should have a go at making bisque with them (see page 100).

To drink: Ice-cold French rosé from Faugères

ingredients

Serves 4 as a simple main course

$^3/_4$ cup butter
8 large garlic cloves, finely chopped
2 lb 4 oz/1 kg cooked shrimp, shells on
large handful of parsley, finely chopped
salt and pepper
crusty bread, to serve

method

Take a very large skillet or large saucepan, place over low heat, and add the butter. When the butter has melted, add the garlic and gently fry for 5 minutes, stirring every now and then.

When the garlic looks like it's about to brown, add the shrimp and gently stir them through the butter. Increase the heat to medium, cover, and cook, shaking the skillet occasionally, for 3 minutes. Add the parsley and cook for an additional 2 minutes. Add plenty of salt and pepper and transfer to a large bowl.

Place in the middle of the table with a bowl for empty shells. Serve with bread for mopping up the butter.

Using cooked shrimp

When you buy pink shrimp, they have already been cooked. People often make the mistake of double-cooking, especially on grills, and the tragic outcome of this is small, rubber shrimpy bullets with a crisp, tasty, but utterly pointless shell. This is to be avoided at all costs! These shrimp need little more than reheating. If you buy frozen shrimp, they should be thawed and thoroughly drained.

This recipe is for cooked shrimp, but works wonderfully with raw shrimp, too. When you buy black or see-through shrimp, they are raw, and should be carefully (but not overly) cooked. As they heat, the shells will turn pink in much the same way that a lobster or a crab shell will.

⑦⑧ Marinated fresh tuna salad

If you manage to lay your hands on a truly wonderful hunk of tuna (or salmon), this is what you should do with it. It's a simple marinade that magically enhances the fish's natural flavors, and the tuna is raw when eaten, so make sure that you're buying sushi-grade stuff. This is easy to make, but if you want the full experience, you will need to buy some ingredients, such as konbu seaweed and bonito flakes, which you can find in Japanese or Chinese stores.

You may have noticed that this book, like all the world's best recipe books, has few newly invented recipes, but is really an encyclopedia of great dishes that have been tried and tested by the world's cooks for thousands of years. In fact, when you speak to any food writers with their heads screwed on, they rarely claim that any recipe is theirs alone. At some point and in some kitchen around the world, pretty much every combination and method has been tried and either enjoyed or rejected. This recipe is different: It's one of mine, and if anything like it has appeared anywhere else, drop me a line and I'll get the lawyers on the case.

The best place in the world to buy tuna is Tsukiji Fish Market in Tokyo, but for an outsider it's a terrifying experience. I managed to buy (only semi-legally) the finest piece of tuna I'd ever seen from a "middle-man" trader, and I decided to make a dish that I would try out on the world's greatest tuna experts: The porters who ferry the tuna around Tsukiji, driving crazy little barrel-shaped transporters around the market. I set up my little tabletop burner on the side of the river and brewed my marinade, then tried it out on the brusque porters. They were all a little surprised to see me offering handfuls of marinated tuna, but they all declared it *oishi*, or "delicious." Phew.

To drink: Pinot Gris or Gewürztraminer floral white wine

ingredients

Serves 4 as a rich appetizer or with sushi rice
for a main course

1 lb 2 oz/500 g fresh tuna or salmon

2 tbsp rice vinegar

1 tbsp sake

$^1/_2$ tbsp sugar

1 tsp soy sauce

piece of dried konbu seaweed, 4 x 6 inches/
10 x 15 cm (optional)

1 tbsp mirin (optional)

1 tbsp bonito flakes (optional)

9 oz/250 g delicate salad greens, such as pea
shoots, arugula, or watercress

crusty bread, to serve

method

Cut the fish into 1-inch/2.5-cm cubes, place in a bowl,
and set aside.

In a small saucepan, mix together all the remaining
ingredients, except the salad greens. Heat gently and
stir to dissolve. Let cool for 10 minutes, remove the
pan from the heat, and pour the contents through
a strainer into a bowl. Add the fish, cover, and let
marinate for 10–20 minutes at room temperature.

Lay some salad greens on individual plates, remove the
fish from the marinade, and lay on top of the greens,
then drizzle over some extra marinade. Serve with
crusty bread.

The fifth taste

Alongside the four commonly known tastes
(salty, sweet, bitter, sour) is the fifth taste:
umami. It's a little odd that no one's come up
with a decent name for it in the English language,
but the nearest word we have is "savoriness."
It's the taste you get from the naturally
occurring glutamate found in large amounts in
many of our foods, such as Parmesan cheese,
roasted chicken, and ripe tomatoes, and, in higher
concentrations than any other food, konbu
seaweed. This recipe uses konbu and bonito
flakes to naturally enhance the flavor of the
tuna, and by God, it's good.

⑦⑨ Grilled herby sardines with lemon

What is a sardine?

A lot of different types of fish are referred to as "sardines" around the world, but most of the sardina and sardinella subspecies range in size from 5 inches/12 cm to around 12 inches/30 cm. Basically, a sardine is a small pilchard—a species high in fat and ideal for canning. Although canned sardines are seen as cheap protein, they keep their flavor very well, and are wonderful when mashed and spread on bread. In common with canned tuna, there are some varieties that are seen as great delicacies, and command high prices in Spain and France.

These beautiful little fish are a real summer classic, and always remind me of eating al fresco on seaside vacations. They have such a big, rich, and, well, fishy flavor, and whenever I cook them they produce the sorts of smells that fill my head with sunshine.

Sardines are criminally cheap to buy, very easy to cook, and extremely healthy to eat, so what are you waiting for? Ah, I know: They have a reputation for being bony and smoky to cook. Well, I have to hold my hands up and say that both are true to some extent, but there are ways of coping with these problems. And if you persevere, you get a great return on the investment of your time.

The boniness of sardines can be dealt with by the right size of sardine—the small and large fish have a much easier bone structure—or by buying sardine fillets.

And the smoke issue? Well, firstly, make sure you aren't cooking the fish straight from the refrigerator, so that the skin doesn't burn too much before it's cooked, and put your extractor fan onto high power. Secondly, keep a really good eye on the broiling. You need the skin to sear a little to get that fresh-broiled flavor, but they shouldn't blacken and burn. Even better, cook them outside on a grill!

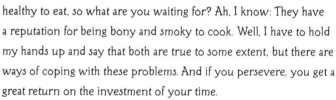

ingredients

Serves 4 as a light lunch

8 sardines, cleaned and scaled
olive oil, for brushing
8 small rosemary sprigs
salt and pepper
lemon wedges and French baguette,
to serve

method

Preheat the broiler to high.

Brush the sardines with oil. Place a rosemary sprig in the cavity of each fish and sprinkle a little salt on top. If you have a fish cage, put the fish into that.

Place under the preheated broiler and cook for 2–3 minutes on each side, until the skin browns a little (be careful not to cook for longer because they can overcook and dry out). Remove from the heat and season with salt and pepper.

Serve on warmed plates with the lemon wedges and bread.

To drink: A citrusy Sauvignon blanc

⑳ Fennel-roasted whole tilapia

Tilapia is one of the oddest-looking edible fish (actually, I won't mince my words: it's ugly) in the ocean. It's thin and spiky, with a huge cantilevered retractable mouth that looks like amateur scaffolding. It's friendless and solitary and it's also a poor swimmer. But when tilapia is delicately and lovingly roasted, it's an absolutely gorgeous fish to eat, with a firm and strong-flavored flesh. As so often with food, the ugliest and oddest-named foods are the most delicious (see Cane Rat, page 160).

I like to serve one entire fish straight from the oven, without filleting or garnishing. I place it in the middle of the table for the sheer spectacle of it all. Everyone dives in with their knives and forks to take what they want, before the fish is flipped over and the feasting begins again. You may have a more delicate approach for your friends (or for any less hardy souls who are put off by seeing a whole fish head, bless 'em), and this can easily be done, too. The tilapia bone structure is clear and strong, so it's easy to fillet them without making a mess. You'll need a pretty large fish, though, because about 60 percent of the body weight is made up of the head and guts. Bake the fish whole and reserve all those bones for making a great fish stock afterward—you can freeze it for later use. Smaller tilapia can be served one per person, too.

Incidentally, this cooking method works for all kinds of whole fish, including salmon, trout, mackerel, and sea bass. You'll need loads of foil!

ingredients

Serves 4 as a main course

1 large tilapia, about 2 kg/4 lb 8 oz, cleaned
but on the bone

4 garlic cloves, roughly chopped

4 bay leaves

2 sprigs fresh thyme

handful of fresh parsley

1 large fennel bulb, sliced and fronds
reserved

2 lemons, sliced

5 tbsp butter, thinly sliced, plus extra
for greasing

generous ¹/₃ cup white wine

salt and pepper

boiled potatoes and steamed vegetables,
to serve

Biblical fish

These fish have a dark spot on their side, which makes them look like a bizarre disembodied eye when seen side on. This eye is shown to potential predators to warn them off, but a French legend says that the dark spot is St. Peter's thumbprint, due to the fact that St. Peter (heaven's gatekeeper) brought a fish—possibly this one—to Jesus.

method

Preheat the oven to 375°F/190°C. Wash the fish and pat dry inside and out. Season with salt and pepper and put 2 garlic cloves, 2 bay leaves, one third of the herbs, and 6 slices of lemon inside the cavity.

Lay two large sheets of foil on top of each other (they should be wide enough to double wrap the whole fish), and grease with butter to prevent the fish from sticking to it. Pull the sides up a little so the ingredients don't spill. Place half of the remaining herbs, lemon slices, fennel slices, and butter slices on the foil and lay the fish on top. Scatter the remaining herbs, lemon, fennel, and butter on top, pour over the wine, and season with salt and pepper.

Wrap the fish loosely, folding over the ends of the foil. Put the package in a roasting pan, place in the preheated oven, and bake for 30–40 minutes.

Open the package at the table (watch out for the steam) and serve with steamed vegetables and potatoes. Let everyone serve themselves from one side—the meat comes away from the bones very easily (don't forget the cheeks)—then turn the fish over and repeat.

**To drink:
Saint-Veran
white Burgundy**

9. From the field

From the field

Let's face it, vegetarian dishes have had a rough ride over the last few decades, always sprinkled with the out-of-date-spice-jar odor of worthy wholesomeness. All attempts at reinvention, the glossy new recipe books, and promotion by celebrities just seemed to be a confirmation of the idea that vegetarian food is deeply uncool.

Even my favorite poet, Andrew Marvell (not known for unfairly dishing the dirt), was heard taking a pop at veggies way back in the mid-1600s in the otherwise marvelous "To His Coy Mistress":

"My vegetable love should grow

Vaster than empires, and more slow."

He can be a bit opaque, can Andy, so I'll translate: basically he's accusing vegetables of being unsexy.

All this is set to change, however, with vegetarian food on the verge of beating seven shades of lunch out of meat, and it seems ironic that this change is rooted in the fact that meat has become so popular. Hoisted by its own carnivorous petard, if you will. For anyone who's been too busy to read the papers recently, I'll explain: there's a world food crisis looming, and the world's meat is, in relative terms, becoming very scarce indeed.

The trouble is that a large proportion of the world's grain resources are used as animal feed, a system that has worked fairly well—until now. Big changes are afoot because newly wealthy India and China have developed a new taste for meat, as well as the purchasing power to buy it. A change in eating habits may sound like a small thing, but when that change involves a combined population of 2.5 billion souls and 37 percent of the entire population of the world, big changes are inevitable.

All of the feed that's needed for raising cows, pigs, and sheep is grown on a relatively static amount of arable land, and when more is needed for feeding animals, two things happen: firstly, land traditionally used for growing food for human consumption is given over to growing animal feed, distorting the market and causing problems around the world. Secondly, the rising demand allows producers to charge more for both meat and vegetables. Basically, vegetables become expensive, but meat even more so.

The new global consciousness of the problems associated with rising meat consumption, coupled with the inescapable fact that meat is more and more expensive, means that vegetarian food is becoming very cool indeed. Eating habits take a while to change, but this is a situation that isn't going to go away, so instead of moaning and wringing our hands, we should react with excitement and a new sense of adventure. It's time to start anew and discover (or at least rediscover) new foods and new ways of eating.

So these ten vegetable-based dishes are racy and delicious, and even, occasionally, interactive. The Tapenade recipe is a simple, messy, hands-on affair, and I always lay on the spread for Hand-made Pizza when I have any celebrated chefs or food writers around for supper, mainly because it puts the creative responsibility firmly into their hands and leaves me to see to the wine. The real Ratatouille should be a revelation to anyone who grew up hating the dish in the 1970s, and the Thai Tom Yum Soup and Whole Artichoke dishes should blow away the aura of wholesome, chaste dullness that clouds vegetarian food, because they are so damn sexy!

81 Tapenade

This is a simple, pungent olive paste that has loads of different uses. It's great spread on toast as a bruschetta appetizer, but it's also fantastic as a dressing for green beans and boiled potatoes, and even as a pesto-like pasta sauce. My favorite way to eat it is to dip crudités in this instead of the usual mayonnaise and it's also extraordinarily good with hard-cooked eggs. My daughters love it eaten straight from the finger, which makes me smile, but makes Grandma Gates frown.

The dish, if you can call something as easy as this a dish, originated in Provence, southern France, and the name comes from *tapeno*, the Provençal word for "caper." It has a robust, earthy taste and you can add your favorite herbs to it without fear of upsetting the balance. I love adding fresh thyme to it, but then I love adding fresh thyme to most things, and often have to be restrained by my wife who complains of "lumps of the garrigue" interfering with her enjoyment of the food. She's probably right.

You can use any olives for this, but I find that the best are the large, dark purple kalamata variety because they have such tender flesh and they are easy to pit. Provençal lucques olives are also great for green tapenade, but they are very expensive.

Olives

Mediterranean olives look most beautiful when picked straight from the tree in late November—my personal favorites are a mixture of green and bruise purple. But I'm afraid you can't eat them fresh because they contain a glucoside substance that makes them unpalatably bitter. The way I prepare them is to wash, then make a small slit in each olive, then soak them in a heavy salt solution for three months. The brine preserves the olives, but also helps with fermentation, breaking down the sugar into lactic acid, which makes them taste so good. You need to change the solution every four weeks, and weigh the olives down with something so they always sit under the brine. Oh, and leave a gap in the lid, otherwise the gases produced by the fermentation will build up until it pops!

To drink: A strong
Belgian **Trappist** beer

Bagna cauda

This translates as "hot bath," an Italian favorite from Piedmont, and it's very similar to Tapenade in that it's pungent and garlicky but contains no olives. It's a garlic and anchovy mixture served hot, like a fondue. Combine milk-poached garlic cloves with anchovies, cream, butter, and olive oil and dip chunks of raw vegetables, such as red bell peppers, cucumber, carrot, fennel, asparagus, and celery, into it.

ingredients

Serves 8 as an appetizer

14 oz/400 g olives, pitted

2 tbsp capers

2 tsp Dijon mustard

juice of $1/2$ lemon

1 garlic clove, finely chopped

12 canned anchovy fillets, drained and soaked to remove the salt

handful of fresh parsley

2 tbsp fresh thyme, chopped (optional)

$2/3$ cup extra virgin olive oil

salt and pepper

rounds of French bread or ciabatta and crudités, to serve

method

Put all the ingredients except the salt and pepper into a food processor and pulse until you get a good paste. Don't make it too smooth—it should retain a little roughness.

Season to taste, bearing in mind that it may already be salty from the capers, olives, and anchovies.

Serve in small bowls with bread and crudités.

⃝82 Risotto primavera

This is a perfect marriage of contrasting textures. On the one hand you get the smooth, creamy, comforting risotto and, on the other, all the freshest, sweetest spring vegetables you can lay your hands on that give a crunch and bite. The key to making risotto is patience, stirring, and more patience.

There's no doubt that this is fantastic cooked in spring when vegetables such as asparagus are young and tender. I know that a lot of food writers put a lot of emphasis on seasonality, and I applaud the theory, but it would be a little too draconian to insist you only cook this in spring. In fact, vegetables like peas are invariably better when frozen because they spend less time breaking down their natural sugars.

ingredients
Serves 4 as a substantial main course

7 oz/200 g asparagus

1 zucchini

7 oz/200 g green beans

1³/₄ cups shelled fresh or frozen peas

2 tbsp olive oil

1 large onion, finely chopped

generous 1 cup risotto rice

scant 3 cups warm chicken stock

3¹/₂ tbsp Vermouth or white wine

handful chopped parsley

1 tbsp fresh thyme leaves

5 tbsp butter

1¹/₄ cups grated Parmesan cheese, plus extra to serve

salt and pepper

Other vegetables

This risotto can easily be made with spinach, artichokes, fava beans, and broccoli in place of the vegetables listed. Just add them at the end of the rice cooking time (1 minute for spinach, 3 minutes for broccoli, etc.).

method

Prepare the green vegetables: Chop the asparagus into bite-size portions, cut the zucchini diagonally into finger-thick slices, trim the beans.

Bring a large saucepan of lightly salted water to a boil, add the green vegetables, and blanch for 1 minute, then remove and drain.

Place a large heavy-bottom saucepan over medium heat, add the olive oil and the onions, and cook them gently for about 10 minutes, until softened. Add the rice and fry, stirring it into the oil for 2 minutes. Reduce the heat, add a ladleful of stock, and stir it into the rice as it absorbs. Gradually add more stock as each ladleful is absorbed. Check the rice—it should be slightly hard in the middle (you may need a little more or less of the liquid). Add the last ladle of stock, the Vermouth, and the herbs, and cook for an additional 5 minutes.

Add the butter, cheese, and blanched vegetables, check the seasoning, and heat through, stirring gently.

Serve in warmed bowls, with Parmesan cheese to sprinkle on top.

The risotto story

The first published risotto recipes appeared in Italy in the mid-nineteenth century, written by the first Italian celebrity food writer and famous chef, Pellegrino Artusi. The dish originated in the rice-growing areas of northern Italy and it's the Italian version of paella or pilaf. The rice used is one of several very specific varieties, all medium- or long-grain. It's assumed to have been a peasant dish that became more and more sophisticated, and these days chefs have experimented with all sorts of ingredients, including sweet ingredients and fruit. One of my favorites, other than this one, is roasted pumpkin risotto.

To drink: White Trebbiano or, if you're feeling frisky, a sparkling Prosecco

⑧③ Whole artichokes with lemon & thyme butter

This dish is all about playing with your food. It's loads of fun, it's sloppy and messy, and it's completely delicious. Kids love eating this way, and it's also one of my wife's favorite dishes of all time.

When chefs use artichokes in their cooking, they generally throw away all the leaves that surround the tender choke at the center of the artichoke, and it's a tragic waste, because there's a huge amount of deliciousness in the leaves you rip off on the way there.

How to eat a whole artichoke

Once the artichoke has cooled enough to be handled, place it flower-side up in the middle of a shallow bowl. Starting from the outside, pull each leaf off, dipping the tender, paler flesh at the bottom into your vinaigrette, then bite off the soft flesh. You scrape it off with your teeth and discard the rest of the leaf. Keep eating the leaves until they get too small to get any flesh from once you're near the middle. This is when the fun starts. Pull out all of the remaining leaves and, using a spoon or flat-bladed knife, pull and carefully scrape out all of the little choke spines in the middle (they are inedible). The remaining flesh is the jewel in the artichoke's crown. Chop it and dip it in the remaining butter.

ingredients

Serves 4

2 lemons
4 large globe artichokes
2 cups plus 2 tbsp butter
2 tbsp fresh thyme leaves
zest and juice of 1 lemon
salt and pepper
crusty bread, to serve

Artichoke lesson

These magnificent-looking vegetables grow in artichoke beds and, although they take up a lot of space and grow very high, each plant can produce a lot of chokes. They look a little like overgrown thistles, which isn't surprising because this is effectively what they are. Interestingly, however, they are not related to Jerusalem artichokes, which are neither artichokes, nor from Jerusalem, but are relatives of the sunflower. They have a sweet, nutty taste but have a (justified) reputation for causing flatulence. Which is why I love serving them to my friends!

method

Fill a large saucepan halfway with cold water. Halve the lemons, squeeze the juice into the water, and drop the skins in, too. Cut the stalks off the artichokes near the base, then "scalp" them by chopping off the top 1 inch/2.5 cm of the leaves. Add them to the water, cover, and bring to a boil. Once boiling, the artichokes will take 20–30 minutes to cook, depending on their tenderness and size. They are ready when the outer leaves can be pulled off without any effort.

Drain the artichokes, turn them upside down, and let cool for 15 minutes while you make your lemon and thyme butter. Gently melt the butter in a small saucepan, and mix in the thyme, lemon zest and juice, and salt and pepper.

Place the artichokes in a shallow bowl and season with salt and pepper. Pour the butter into small bowls—either individually or to share. Put a large bowl in the middle of the table for discarded artichoke parts and leaves. Serve with bread for mopping up.

To drink: Sancerre white wine

⑧⑷ Ratatouille

In the right hands, ratatouille is a wonderful expression of the bounty of the land, but in the wrong hands it's a criminal offense. When I was a child, ratatouille abuse was rife. Meals across the world that had been made with love and sincerity were cruelly and systematically destroyed by a slop of wet vegetables seeping across the plate. At one point there was even a moment of moral confusion when I was thinking about becoming a vegetarian, but from which I was saved (thank God) by the horrific sight of a slurry of tomatoes and damp zucchini that flooded out an otherwise delicious couscous salad.

But redemption for ratatouille has come from an unlikely corner: Hollywood. If you haven't already seen it, the movie *Ratatouille* features a supertaster rat who takes over a Michelin-starred kitchen and, for the most important meal of his life, he cooks the humble dish of the title, melting the heart of the most evil restaurant critic the world has ever known. Not only did the film resurrect the dish in our consciousness, it also drew attention to the fact that it can be cooked amazingly well, if you try.

So what is ratatouille? It's a ragout of onions, tomatoes, eggplant, zucchini, and bell peppers, all cooked separately to begin with, then roasted in olive oil to intensify their wondrous flavors. But then you probably know all that already. What you might not know is that it's best made the day before, and served at room temperature, or just warmer.

ingredients

Serves 4 as a simple lunch

3 red bell peppers

generous ³/₄ cup olive oil

1 zucchini, thickly sliced

1 fennel bulb, roughly chopped

2 large red onions, roughly sliced

3 white onions, thickly sliced

2 large eggplants, thickly sliced

1 lb 5 oz/600 g ripe tomatoes, blanched, peeled, cored, and seeded

1 large tbsp fresh thyme leaves

1 large tbsp fresh rosemary leaves

1 tsp sugar

salt and pepper

crusty bread and butter, to serve

To drink: A nice oaky Chardonnay

method

Preheat the broiler to high, then place the red bell peppers on the broiler pan and place under the heat until the skins blacken. Turn and broil again, continuing until they are blackened all over. Put them in a bowl and cover with plastic wrap to sweat for 10 minutes, then peel them under cold running water. Cut them open and seed them, then chop the flesh into large chunks.

Meanwhile, place a large heavy-bottom saucepan over medium heat and add half the oil. Add the zucchini and fry until it begins to brown. Transfer it to a large roasting pan and keep warm. Add the fennel and onions to the pan and fry for 15–20 minutes, until they soften, then transfer them to the roasting pan. Add the eggplants and some more oil (they will soak up a lot) and fry until they begin to brown. Add them to the roasting pan, laid flat in a single layer.

Preheat the oven to 375°F/190°C. Add the tomatoes, red bell peppers, thyme, and rosemary to the roasting pan and distribute the vegetables evenly across it. Sprinkle the sugar over the whole lot and gently mix through. There should be one layer of vegetables, not a stew. If you need more room, use two roasting pans. Season with salt and pepper, drizzle with olive oil, and place, uncovered, in the preheated oven for 40–50 minutes, until they start to brown.

Refrigerate overnight or eat immediately with crusty bread and butter.

85 Roasted pumpkin, garlic & thyme soup

This is a classic thick, robust, full-flavored soup. You can serve it in the summer with a traditional soupy consistency, but in the winter I also enjoy it cooked with half the stock and so thick that your spoon stands up in it.

Pumpkins are extraordinary vegetables, with so much sugar in them that they can sometimes be used as a replacement for fruit. When they are cooked long and slow, the sugar in both pumpkins and garlic caramelizes and creates a deep, soothing flavor. The odd thing is that while the garlic becomes gentler in flavor, the pumpkin intensifies—it's so strong and delicious that roasted pumpkin can be used as a replacement for sausage or bacon in some recipes.

Pumpkin bowls

In the middle of the season, when pumpkin is cheap and plentiful, it's fun to buy some extra small ones to use as serving bowls. Cut off a thin slice from the bottom to flatten it out so it doesn't fall over, then cut a lid off the top, scoop out the innards, and ladle in the soup. There are two approaches to this: If you have good carving skills, you can extract the flesh and use that to make your soup, but if it's too tricky, save the bowls and roast them after use. If you don't use it straight away, keep the roasted pulp in your refrigerator to add to salads and pastas, or freeze it for use later.

Uses for a roasted pumpkin

Shred it and add it to cooked tagliatelle with some sour cream, fresh thyme, a little chopped chile, and plenty of good olive oil. It's also fantastic to add to salads—both heavy ones, such as potato salad or beet, or lighter ones using endive leaves. It also makes fantastic chutney. And what about all those pumpkin seeds? Not my bag, unless roasted and covered in so much salt that you may as well be eating toasted almonds, which are leagues ahead.

method

Preheat the oven to 375°F/190°C. Take two pieces of foil large enough to wrap a garlic bulb and place a bulb in the middle of each. Pour ¹/₂ tablespoon of olive oil over each, season with salt and pepper, wrap, and place in a large roasting pan. Peel the pumpkin, then cut into large chunks. Toss the chunks in the remaining olive oil, some salt and pepper, and half of the thyme leaves. Place in the roasting pan in a single layer and roast, uncovered, for 1 hour.

Meanwhile, place a large heavy-bottom saucepan over medium heat, add the butter, and melt. Add the onion and cook, stirring occasionally, until softened. Add the flour and cook it through for 2 minutes. Add the stock, a few spoonfuls at a time to begin with, then add all of it.

When the pumpkin is browned remove it from the oven, add to the stock, bring to a simmer, and simmer for 10 minutes. Open the garlic packages and let cool. When cool enough to touch, break up the bulbs, place the cloves on a cutting board, and squeeze down on each until the softened garlic squeezes out.

Remove the soup from the heat and carefully blend in small batches in a food processor with the garlic and the remaining thyme.

Pour into bowls, drop a spoonful of sour cream on top, then drizzle over a little oil and serve.

ingredients

Serves 6 for lunch or as a substantial appetizer

2 whole garlic bulbs

4 tbsp olive oil, plus extra for drizzling

2 lb/900 g pumpkin or butternut squash

2 tbsp fresh thyme leaves

2 tbsp butter

1 large onion, finely chopped

1 tbsp all-purpose flour

5 cups chicken stock

generous ¹/₃ cup sour cream

salt and pepper

To drink: A spicy Pinot Noir

⑧⑥ Gazpacho

This legendary Spanish cold soup is a gourmet's lifeline—a way of escaping the crushing midsummer Mediterranean sunshine and having lunch at the same time. It really is an expression of all the best salads that the Spanish make, but mixed together in a deliciously fresh and piquant soup.

Cold soups can be disastrous if you don't season and flavor them well, because heat is essential for releasing and agitating the flavor molecules that we love so much. It's important to taste the soup before you serve it, and don't be surprised if you need to add more salt and pepper than usual (it's still likely to be far less than you'd find in any type of canned soup).

There are thousands of recipes for gazpacho, but the crucial thing is to make it with well-flavored tomatoes. No amount of seasoning, chile, or hope will pump flavor into one of those dreaded pale, firm "salad tomatoes." And you can't cut corners just because you think they are going to be finely chopped. In their song "The End," the Beatles said "And in the end, the love you take is equal to the love you make." In other words: "You'll get a fantastic lunch if you give the vegetable man loads of money." At least, I think that's what they meant.

Lettuce soups

Lettuce soup tastes nicely of cut grass, but if you make it remember that you need a lot to produce a little flavor so don't add too much water and don't use too strong a stock.

ingredients

Serves 4 as a refreshing appetizer

1 red bell pepper, cored, seeded, and chopped

2 lb 4 oz/1 kg ripe tomatoes, cored and chopped

2 tbsp very finely chopped onion

3 garlic cloves, crushed

1 cucumber, peeled and chopped

$3^1/_2$ slices stale bread, crumbled

3 tbsp red wine vinegar or sherry vinegar

$3^1/_2$ tbsp olive oil, plus extra for drizzling

ice cubes (optional)

salt and pepper

To drink: A fine Manzanilla sherry

method

Set aside a handful of the red bell pepper, a handful of the tomatoes, and half the chopped onion in the refrigerator. Put the rest in a food processor with the garlic, cucumber, and the remaining onion and puree until smooth. Add the bread, vinegar, and oil and blend again. Season with salt and pepper to taste. If the soup is too thick, add some ice, then place in the refrigerator for 2 hours.

When ready to serve, check the vinegar and seasoning and ladle into bowls. Scatter over the reserved red bell pepper, tomatoes, and onions, then drizzle over a swirl of olive oil. Serve.

87 Thai tom yum soup with fish

Tom yum is a justifiably famous, bracing,
hot and sour combination of all the best flavors that Thai food
has to offer. It's a clean-tasting, fragrant, healthy broth with a hit of chile,
and a whack of lime juice to bring it all to life. There are many variations on the
accompanying ingredients—you can add shrimp, chicken, and fish, and any mixture of
thinly sliced vegetables, but it should really remain a head-clearing broth with extra parts
floating in it, rather than a stew.

There are a number of ingredients in the list, but if you want to dip your toe in the broth before
stocking up at the Thai supermarket, you can always try out the instant version first (see below).

Instant tom yum soup

You can buy pretty decent jars of tom yum paste, and they do create (almost)
instant meals if you're feeling seriously lazy. The instructions on my jar read: "Put
2 spoonfuls of paste in 3 cups of boiling water and add shrimp and mushrooms as
required." And that's it. I would suggest that you add any vegetables you have on
hand, after thinly slicing them first, and that you should not be tempted to
fry the paste as with Indian spice pastes (this will make it taste acrid).
Simmer any fresh ingredients for 2 minutes, but that's it. The
paste is made with (among other things) lemongrass, chile,
galangal, and kaffir lime leaves, all of which can be hard
to track down if you live far from Thai or
Chinese stores, so it's worth trying
this shortcut.

ingredients

Serves 6 as a light main course

5¹/₂ cups light chicken stock

6 lemongrass stalks, crushed to release
their flavor

3 tbsp very finely chopped cilantro roots

10 kaffir lime leaves, central stalks torn off

1 red chile, seeded and finely chopped

1-inch/2.5-cm piece of galangal (or fresh
ginger), peeled and thinly sliced

3 tbsp nam pla

1 tbsp sugar

1 lb 2 oz/500 g shrimp, shelled
except for the tails

1 lb 2 oz/500 g firm white fish, such as cod or
monkfish, chopped into bite-size pieces

8 oz/225 g canned bamboo shoots or
water chestnuts

12 cherry tomatoes, halved

juice of 2 limes

handful of fresh cilantro leaves and handful of
fresh basil leaves (Thai basil if you can find it),
chopped, to garnish

**To drink: Large bottles
of Thai Elephant beer**

method

Pour the stock into a large saucepan and add the
lemongrass, cilantro roots, lime leaves, chile, galangal,
nam pla, and sugar. Cover the saucepan. Bring to a boil,
then reduce the heat and simmer for 10 minutes.

Add the shrimp, fish, and bamboo shoots and simmer
for an additional 4 minutes. Add the tomatoes and lime
juice and check the seasoning, adding more fish sauce
and sugar, if necessary.

Remove and discard the lemongrass stalks, then divide
the soup between six bowls and scatter over the
cilantro and basil leaves.

⑧⑧ Mezze of hummus, herbed tabbouleh & smoky baba ganoush

Mezze is a Middle Eastern and North African version of tapas. The best mezze I ever ate was in the tiny Arabic village of Yanun in the Occupied West Bank, made by a family who had a few olive trees and goats. They cured their own chile olives, pressed their own oil, made their own cheese, and used any surplus to barter for chickpeas. They also made their own flatbread in their taboon underground oven. I'm not suggesting for a moment that you need a herd of goats and an olive grove to make fantastic-tasting mezze, but you definitely don't need expensive ingredients.

The word *mezze* means "taste" or "relish," and it's a fantastic way to eat—especially for someone like me who loves to pick at and play with my food, experimenting with flavors and textures. I serve mezze with little bowls of olive oil and za'atar (a mixture of ground thyme with sesame seeds, sumac, and salt). Dip the bread into the oil and then the herbs, and eat it. Delicious.

Other mezze suggestions

There are no rules to mezze, and it's always fun to mix a few store-bought dishes with some you make yourself. Try adding some plates of taramasalata, falafels, stuffed vine leaves, feta cheese, or broiled haloumi cheese, broiled bell peppers, and mild chiles.

To drink: Cardamom coffee
(afterward, of course)

ingredients

Serves 10 as an appetizer

Hummus

14 oz/400 g canned chickpeas, drained
1 garlic clove, crushed
3 tbsp tahini
pinch of salt
juice of 1 lemon
4 tbsp olive oil, plus extra for drizzling
small handful of parsley, chopped

Herbed tabbouleh

$3^1/_2$ oz/100 g fine bulgur wheat
1 lb/450 g cherry tomatoes, halved
3 bunches parsley, finely chopped
2 bunches fresh mint, finely chopped
zest and juice of 1 lemon
1 garlic clove, crushed
4 tbsp olive oil
salt and pepper

Smoky baba ganoush

4 eggplants
3 garlic cloves, crushed
3 tbsp tahini
5 tbsp olive oil
salt and pepper

method

Place the chickpeas, reserving a handful, with 2 tablespoons of water in a food processor and blend. Add the garlic, tahini, salt, lemon juice, and olive oil and blend for at least 2 minutes to a smooth, fine paste, adding more water, if necessary. Crush the reserved chickpeas with the back of a fork and add to the paste.

Transfer to a plate or wide bowl and stir in the chopped parsley, then spread out with the back of a spoon so that the surface will hold shallow splashes of olive oil. Pour extra oil over the top and serve.

Put the bulgur wheat into a strainer, soak it with water, and let drain for 5 minutes. If it still feels dry, soak and let drain once more.

Mix with the remaining ingredients in a large bowl, season with salt and pepper, and serve.

Preheat the oven to 425°F/220°C. Prick the eggplants all over with a fork, then hold them over a gas flame using a pair of metal tongs until the skins char and blister. Place them in a roasting pan and roast in the preheated oven for 35–55 minutes, until they are soft inside. Set aside to cool.

When cool, slice the eggplants in half and scoop out the flesh into a bowl using a spoon. Add the remaining ingredients, season with salt and pepper, mash with a fork, and serve.

89 Quirky hand-made pizzas

Pizza history

Pizzas will forever be associated with Naples in southern Italy, but have spread around the world to become one of our most loved fast foods. Dishes of bread topped with other ingredients and then baked are found across the world, including the famous Welsh Rarebit. The word "pizza" cropped up as early as AD 997, and its fame spread across Italy. The original Neapolitan pizzas were a simple marinara, using tomato, garlic, oregano, and oil, and the Margherita (named in honour of the Italian queen's visit to Naples) of tomato, mozzarella cheese, and fresh basil leaves.

There's no better meal than one made by your friends and family themselves. Getting everyone to make their own pizzas is a guaranteed recipe for hilarity, but there are other benefits too: Everyone gets a bespoke meal, any dietary issues are competently dealt with, and, in any case, why should you do all the work?

Basically, you provide all the key ingredients for everyone to build their own pizzas: Dough, tomato sauce, and a good variety of toppings. You can be as generous or as thrifty as you like (some of the world's best pizzas are the simplest ones) and it's a wonderful meal if you've got chefs or food fanatics coming around for dinner, because you never have to expose your own cooking skills to criticism.

This is a fantastic two-course meal, because as soon as everyone's made their first pizzas, some of the ingredients left on the table can be eaten as antipasti. But when everyone's ready to build their own personal creation, it's worth giving a few words of advice:

1. The thinner the base, the better it will cook (unless you're lucky enough to have your own ferociously hot wood-fired pizza oven).

2. Start with a light spreading of tomato sauce and some mozzarella cheese and then add your toppings and a little olive oil.

3. Keep the pizza pretty dry—soggy ingredients spell disaster.

4. Less is more! If you add too many ingredients, it will be a cacophony of flavors. If people want to play with flavors, try doing different combinations in each quarter of the pizza.

ingredients

Serves 6 as an antipasti and main course

5 tsp active dry yeast

1³/₄ cups lukewarm water

¹/₂ tsp salt

3 tbsp oil

5³/₄ cups all-purpose flour or Italian 00 flour, plus extra for dusting

generous 2¹/₂ cups tomato sauce

choice of toppings from the following:

prepared artichoke hearts

14 oz/400 g mozzarella cheese, thinly sliced

herbs (basil, thyme, rosemary)

red bell peppers

grilled eggplants and zucchini

semolina flour, for sprinkling

olive oil, for drizzling

method

Mix the yeast with the water and add the salt and oil. Mix four fifths of the flour into the water using a fork, until you have a good doughy texture (add the rest of the liquid only if you think the dough needs it). Sprinkle some flour on a counter and knead the dough for 3 minutes. Put it into a bowl, cover, and let rise in a warm place for 1 hour.

You can put the toppings in little bowls and spread them out on the table to be eaten as antipasti, but you'll need pizza toppings, so warn your guests not to finish them all off! Preheat the oven to 450°F/230°C.

Knead the dough for an additional 8 minutes and then divide into 12 balls. Give one each to your guests, saving the remainder for a second round of pizzas. Each ball will be sufficient for one small–medium pizza. Sprinkle three baking sheets with semolina flour. Tell everyone to stretch out the dough as thinly as possible, then spread some tomato sauce over the top. They should then lay their chosen ingredients on top, cover with mozzarella cheese, and drizzle over a little olive oil.

Place the pizzas in the preheated oven and bake for 10–20 minutes. Serve hot, and make sure everyone has some of each pizza. Once the first batch has been eaten, start again.

To drink: Chianti red wine

⑳ Asparagus & tomato tart

This is a great dish to make for summer picnics and back-yard lunches, perfect to eat with a few bowls of olives, some homemade coleslaw, and a potato salad with chive mayonnaise. The ingredients are interchangeable with other crisp spring and summer vegetables, such as zucchini, baby carrots, spinach, artichoke hearts, and red bell peppers. You do need to have a good tart pan, though, 10–12 inches/ 25–30 cm, preferably loose-bottom, so that you don't mangle the tart when you remove it.

Fake Parmesan

Parmigiano-Reggiano is the area in northern Italy that produces the famous cheese we know as Parmesan. It's a protected designation of origin, and only cheese made in this area can legally be called Parmesan, but there are other areas that produce very similar cheeses, and although purists balk at the idea, some of these Parme-likes are actually great cheeses. There's one made in the southern English county of Sussex that tastes good, deep, and salty, and has been very well matured, but the only problem is that Britain doesn't have the machinery required to cut such a huge, rock-hard slab into usable chunks, so once it has been matured it has to be shipped to Italy for cutting, then shipped back to Britain again for eating.

ingredients

Serves 4 as the main dish at a picnic

13 oz/375 g store-bought shortcrust pastry
butter, for greasing
1 bunch thin asparagus spears
9 oz/250 g spinach leaves
3 large eggs, beaten
$^2/_3$ cup heavy cream
1 garlic clove, crushed
10 small cherry tomatoes, halved
handful fresh basil, chopped
$^1/_4$ cup grated Parmesan cheese
salt and pepper

method

Preheat the oven to 375°F/190°C. Remove the pastry from the refrigerator at least 15 minutes before use, otherwise it may be brittle and difficult to handle. Grease a 10–12-inch/25–30-cm tart pan with butter, then roll out the pastry and line the pan with it. Cut off any excess, prick the bottom with a fork, cover with a piece of wax paper, and fill with dried beans, then bake it for 20–30 minutes, until lightly browned. Remove from the oven and let cool slightly. Reduce the oven temperature to 350°F/180°C.

Meanwhile, bend the asparagus spears until they snap, and discard the woody ends. Bring a large saucepan of water to a boil, add the asparagus, and blanch for 1 minute, then remove and drain. Add the spinach to the boiling water, then remove immediately and drain very well.

Mix the eggs, cream, and garlic together and season with salt and pepper. Lay the blanched spinach at the bottom of the pastry shell, add the asparagus and tomatoes, cut-side up, in any arrangement you like, scatter over the basil, then pour the egg mixture on top. Transfer to the oven and bake for about 35 minutes, or until the filling has set nicely. Sprinkle the Parmesan cheese on top and let cool to room temperature before serving.

To drink: Mâcon Villages white wine

10.Afters

Afters

The pastry chef in a fine restaurant enjoys a strange and eccentric existence, living life as if on an island, removed from the screaming, swirling cacophony of the rest of the kitchen team as it argues and collaborates, struggling through each service as if about to tear itself apart.

But the pastry chef is a law unto himself, living in relative isolation, often working very different hours from the rest of the kitchen because the demand for his craft starts late and ends late in the service. The ones I have met seem to have a Zenlike calm. They are, after all, dealing in the final flourish of the meal (the word "dessert" comes from the French *desservir*, "to clear the table"), the part that is often purely pleasurable and indulgent. And this is why a naughty glint in their eyes twinkles through the Zen.

After the main course has been cleared, the sensible, tasty, yet nutritious fuel has been consumed, and people usually don't—strictly speaking—need any more food. And here is where they enter the dark world of culinary decadence.

You see, the pastry chef's world is a naughty, sensual place of earthly pleasures and happy abandon, a rocky, dissolute shore upon which diets are shipwrecked, a dangerous sea where swirling currents of creamy pleasure sweep away the stiffest anti-cholesterol resolve, a culinary hinterland where the shifting sands of chocolate and sugar trick even the most parsimonious into following the path toward luxurious superfluity.

Hey, get me with all my fruity nautical metaphors. That's what desserts do to a man!

So, what of this selection of the ten best? Well, you may argue that I've got it wrong, and I've missed the best cream puffs, bavaroises, mousses, crumbles, pithiviers, and fine cheeses, and of course, you'd be right. There are so many fine, dreamlike sweet indulgences, but my choice of ten is another personal journey through my own experience, although I still think it would be difficult to argue that any of what I've chosen shouldn't be included, from the creamy outrage that is Zabaglione, the classicism of Crème Brûlée, to the down-and-dirty frankness of Sticky Toffee Pudding.

But the real reason that this chapter is called Afters rather than Desserts is because there is one substance on the earth that I love more than any other. Yup, I love CHEESE.

Cheese is one of those extraordinary substances that has to be given birth to, grown, nurtured, gestated, coaxed into life. A fine cheese bears all the olfactory marks of its upbringing, from the bearer of its milk, whether sheep, cow, goat, or yak. A properly nurtured, properly kept artisan cheese will practically taste of the dairyman. I simply can't end an evening without a piece of cheese, even if it's just a sliver or a crumb to remind me that those tastes exist. For me, cheese is one of the crazy, naughty material substances that makes life worth living—indeed, that makes life wonderful. And that's what "afters" should be about: A rare and precious flight of wicked culinary lunacy.

⑨¹ Zabaglione

The name alone makes you salivate, doesn't it? And so it should, seeing as it contains purely naughty ingredients: Egg yolks, sugar, and Marsala. This is one of those dishes that really makes life worth living. It's a dessert de luxe, a heavenly balm for your stressed-out soul.

I've often fantasized about which of my favorite substances I'd choose to bathe in if I had unlimited resources and a limited sense of proportion. Champagne sounds like it might smart a bit, Belazu aged balsamic vinegar might stain, Tokaji wine would have severe health and safety issues, and Tuscan olive oil would make it impossible to get out of the tub. Asses milk doesn't quite hit the nail on the head, although whipped cream wouldn't be a bad idea. I think I'd choose baked beans for the sheer sensory adventure, but as a way to luxuriate in sensory nirvana, I'd choose zabaglione.

This is very simple to cook, but you do need to make up (or buy) a bain-marie (a double-boiler—it's just a bowl or saucepan sitting in another saucepan of hot or boiling water). It's important that the eggs don't scramble, and there's a danger of this happening if you place your saucepan straight on the heat. Incidentally, don't throw the egg whites away—they can be used to make pavlova or meringues.

What can I do with a whole bottle of Marsala?

This is a fortified wine from Sicily. It's a dark amber color and has a heady, portlike flavor. If you don't have a bottle of Marsala in your liquor cabinet, you can try substituting Madeira, port, or Moscato, but I do recommend that you lay your hands on some for a lot of reasons. It's a great wine to go with cheese, but it also makes fantastic gravy for pan-fried steaks. After you've seared some lamb or beef steaks, put them in a warm oven while you deglaze the pan with a hefty splash of Marsala and some thyme leaves. Reduce the liquid by about half, add in any stray juices that have collected under your meat, and pour it over steaks and salad alike. It's wonderful.

ingredients

Serves 6

$^1/_3$ cup superfine sugar

6 egg yolks

$^3/_4$ cup Marsala, Madeira, or other sweet dessert wine

splash of brandy

amaretti cookies, to serve

method

Fill a saucepan halfway with water and bring to a boil. Place a heatproof bowl over the pan so that it doesn't quite touch the boiling water.

Put the sugar and eggs into the bowl and whisk until light and creamy. Add the Marsala a little at a time, whisking continuously, then add the brandy and continue whisking for up to 15 minutes, until you have a floaty, silky foam.

Pour it into bowls and serve with amaretti cookies. It can also be made ahead of time and served chilled.

The zabaglione story

The correct Italian spelling of this dish is zabaione. It was probably invented in the sixteenth century at the Florentine court of the powerful Medici family, but was also popular among the nineteenth-century Russian aristocracy. The French have a version called sabayon. There's also a similar dish called Kogel Mogel in Poland that uses chocolate, honey, or rum.

To drink: Sauternes or Frontignan (sweet French wine)

⑨② Chocolate fondant

There's nothing like chocolate. Naughty, life-affirming, heart-stopping, sweet-bitter, musky chocolate. Its worth going bad for: Breaking your diet, bursting your wallet, or ignoring your doctor. I know more people who have a weakness for chocolate than any other foodstuff.

This is the best way to enjoy chocolate. It's not quite as brash as diving headfirst into a swimming pool of cocoa and cream, but it's not far off.

You need a set of little molds for this—cone-shaped dariole molds are ideal for easy extraction.

Fondant

Literally speaking, fondant is a mixture of sugar and glucose syrup dissolved in water and boiled before being mixed and then kneaded into a smooth white paste. Chocolate fondant is a cheeky variation on the original theme.

Chocolate history

The Mayans of Central America were particularly fond of chocolate, and Mayan dignitaries were often buried with bowls of chocolate to take with them into the afterlife. The Aztecs traded extensively in it and drank a huge amount of it, reserving it for the dignitaries whenever possible, and using it for ceremonies and after dinners. Columbus captured a canoe full of cocoa beans in 1502, but it wasn't until about 20 years later that the Spanish learned what it was really for. It soon arrived in Europe and the public went crazy for it. By the seventeenth century, Italian chefs were using it as a cooking ingredient, the British were drinking it, and it had reached the French court.

Cocoa

Cocoa pods are odd-looking things that hang off the trunk of the cacao tree by a thin stalk. They are large—about two thirds the size of a football—and yellow or red in color. An average tree produces around 30 cocoa pods. The ripe pods are split and the beans and flesh are scraped out and left to stand in the sun to ferment, developing the flavor. The beans are then dried and sent to chocolate manufacturers.

ingredients

Serves 4

$^1/_2$ cup superfine sugar

$^3/_4$ cup butter, plus extra for greasing

6 oz/175 g semisweet chocolate

3 large eggs

3 large egg yolks

1 tbsp all-purpose flour

mint leaves, to decorate

method

Grease 4 dariole molds thoroughly with butter.

Fill a small saucepan halfway with water and bring it to simmering point. Place a heatproof bowl over the pan and add the sugar, butter, and chocolate. Stir until the butter has melted, then remove from the heat.

Whisk until well mixed. Add the eggs and egg yolks and whisk them in. Sift in the flour and fold it in.

Pour the mixture into the molds and put them into the refrigerator for 30 minutes.

Preheat the oven to 425°F/220°C. Put the molds into the oven and bake for 8–10 minutes, then remove. Let rest, then turn out onto serving plates. Place a couple of mint leaves on the top and a few scattered around.

To drink: Oloroso sherry or sweet Greek dessert wine (try it—it's great stuff)

⑨③ Crème brûlée

This is one of France's great gifts to gastronomy. It translates as "burnt cream," which is an unappealing, if accurate, name for a dish that is effectively a fine custard (which the French call crème Anglaise), topped with caramelized sugar. It is traditionally made in individual portions that are slipped under a hot broiler and heated until the sugar caramelizes, then quickly hardens. Each ecstatic recipient cracks the lid on their crème with a wallop of their spoon before delving inside to luxuriate in the creamy center.

The last time I ate this was at dinner with my gorgeous French friend Manon. After the main course, Manon announced that she had made crème brûlée, and a cheer (yes, really) went up from all of us gathered around the table. The crèmes had all been prepared and all that needed to be done was the final brûléeing under the broiler. Manon's husband Jeremy put the little dishes of crème on his broiler pan, lifted it up, and it promptly slipped from his grasp. The fall of the ramekins seemed to happen in slow motion. Our delight turned to dismay, and we shouted a collective "Noooooooooo!" (also in slow motion) as they crashed and smashed. Only one lone crème brûlée remained, jammed between Jeremy's knee and the stove. The six of us shared the one remaining crème, but it was torture because it was spectacularly good and simply reminded us of our tragic gastronomic loss. I'm happy to report that after a mere two months we have nearly—not quite, but very nearly—forgiven Jeremy, and he is hopeful of being allowed back into the kitchen soon.

Let's have a chat about blow torches. You don't have to have one to make crème brûlée, but you need to be able to heat the top really quickly so that you don't cook the custard underneath. This really is best done with one of those little domestic blow torches that you've seen in cook's shops. Go on, you know you've always wanted one

Vanilla

This is essential for making a really good crème brûlée, and it always tastes better if you lay your hands on the real thing than if you use a vanilla extract. The vanilla vine grows upward until waist high, then it's trained back down again and roots from the "top" before coming up again. It does this several times, creating a long, hooplike row. The vine is green, with long, brown leaves and flowers that only open early in the mornings. It is thought that the flowers are pollinated only by humming birds and by one species of bee. The beans are steamed, then left to ferment for several weeks.

ingredients

Serves 8

2¹/₄ cups heavy cream

1 vanilla bean

¹/₂ cup superfine sugar, plus extra
for the topping

6 egg yolks

method

Preheat the oven to 325°F/160°C.

Pour the cream into a small saucepan. Split the vanilla bean in half lengthwise. Scrape the seeds into the pan, then chop the bean into little pieces and add that too. Heat the cream to boiling, then reduce the heat and simmer gently for 5 minutes.

Put the sugar and egg yolks in a heatproof bowl and beat with a spoon until well mixed. Pour the hot cream into the egg mixture, beating (not whisking) as you pour, until it's nicely thickened. Pass this mixture through a fine strainer into another bowl or pitcher. Pour the mixture into a wide, flat dish (or 8 small shallow dishes) and lay this in a roasting pan. Carefully pour some boiling hot water into the pan so that it comes halfway up the sides of the crème brûlée dish or dishes.

Place in the preheated oven and bake for 33–45 minutes, until the custard has just set.

Remove from the oven and let cool to room temperature. Sprinkle over some sugar and then gently caramelize it using a kitchen blow torch, or under a very hot broiler. Let cool for a few minutes, then serve.

To drink: Hungarian Tokaji 5 Puttonyos sweet dessert wine

⑨④ Sticky toffee pudding

The mere mention of this classic, childhood British dessert will cause a sigh of homesickness in even the most resolute Britons, whether they are at home or not. It's essentially a date-based sponge cake that soaks up an outrageously luscious sugary syrup. For many it's the epitome of uncomplicated, simple, childish joy and, as you can tell from its name, it's sweet, sticky, and so outrageously soft that you really don't need to own your own set of teeth to enjoy it.

There are several restaurants that lay claim to the invention of this dish, but its true lineage remains disputed. I suspect it was really invented by a Victorian housekeeper dropping a bowl of molasses or sugar syrup on a sponge cake by mistake (after being startled by a Victorian mouse, perhaps), then putting it aside to devour later with the nanny, only to fall in love with her accidental creation and keep it secret for decades. It certainly isn't a traditional steamed pudding.

The golden age of puddings?

Undoubtedly the reign of Queen Victoria (1837–1901), when Windsor pudding (a lemon-fragranced apple and rice creation) was all the rage, was when sponge-based puddings were at their peak. The cooks of the time played with suet, dried fruit, and different methods of steaming, boiling, and spongification. Although the most famous cookery writer of the period, Mrs. Beeton, didn't write about sticky toffee pudding, she did give recipes for lemon-flavored Everton toffee and hundreds of puddings. Her recipe for Rolled Treacle Pudding contains this disclaimer: "We have inserted this pudding, being economical, and a favorite one with children; it is, of course, only suitable for a nursery, or a very plain family dinner." Heaven forbid that a Victorian lady would admit that it's fabulous!

ingredients

Serves 4

7 oz/200 g pitted dates, finely chopped

1 tsp baking soda

generous $^2/_3$ cup water

scant $^3/_4$ cup butter, plus extra for greasing

1 cup golden superfine sugar

2 eggs

1 tsp vanilla extract

1$^3/_4$ cups self-rising flour

Sauce

$^3/_4$ cup dark brown sugar

2 tbsp butter, cut into chunks

$^1/_4$ cup heavy cream

method

Preheat the oven to 350°F/180°C. Put the dates, baking soda, and water in a saucepan and simmer for 5 minutes until the dates are softened. Set aside.

Beat the butter with the golden superfine sugar until light and fluffy, then beat in the eggs, vanilla extract, and flour, then the dates and their cooking liquid. Grease an 8-inch/20-cm round cake pan or baking dish with a little butter and add the mixture. Cook for about 35 minutes, checking after 20 minutes that it isn't burning. It is ready when a knife inserted into the center comes out clean. It must not dry out!

Meanwhile, to make the sauce, put the brown sugar, butter, and cream into a saucepan and stir over low heat until fully mixed. Increase the heat and boil for 1 minute to thicken. Remove from the heat and keep warm. To serve, place a piece of sponge on each of 4 plates and top with the sauce.

To drink: Australian Orange Muscat dessert wine

Serves 6 as a substantial dessert

1 cup superfine sugar
scant $^3/_4$ cup unsalted butter
1 lb 12 oz/800 g tart apples
12 oz/350 g store-bought puff pastry
vanilla ice cream, to serve

⑨⑤ Tarte tatin

My French friend Manon is the Queen of Puddings, and she once made the best apple pie I ever ate. It was a tarte tatin, the upside-down version invented (or at least, popularized) by the famous Tatin sisters, who ran a restaurant in the village of Lamotte-Beuvron near Orléans. If Manon ever decides to stop designing handbags, she should set up a patisserie.

It's an ingenious approach to making pies: Put the pastry on the top to make it soft and floaty, cook the apples underneath it with sugar and butter, and then turn it over so that the delicious syrupy goo seeps down through the apples and into the lightened pastry. I wonder if it was first made by someone who read a recipe wrongly, and unwittingly stumbled into pie heaven. It matters not because, ye gods, this stuff is good!

Purists and apple tart obsessives can buy themselves the classic shallow copper pan to make this in, but they cost a king's ransom and you can still make a damn fine pie using any decent smallish skillet (preferably steep-sided) that can go in the oven.

method

Place an 8-inch/20-cm ovenproof skillet over low heat and add the sugar. Melt the sugar until it starts to caramelize, but do not let it burn, then add the butter and stir it in to make a light taffy sauce. Remove from the heat.

Peel the apples and cut them into eighths vertically. Core the apples and lay them in the skillet on top of the sauce, cut-side up. They should fill the skillet. If there are any large gaps, add a few more apple pieces. Put the skillet over medium heat and cover. Simmer, without stirring, for about 5–10 minutes, until the apples have soaked up some of the sauce, then remove from the heat.

Preheat the oven to 375°F/190°C. Roll out the pastry so that it will thickly cover the skillet, with extra space on the sides. Lay it on top of the apples and tuck the edges down inside between the fruit and the skillet until it is sealed. Don't worry about making it look too neat—it will be turned over before eating.

Put the skillet into the preheated oven and bake for 25–35 minutes, checking to make sure the pastry doesn't burn. The pastry should be puffed and golden. Remove from the oven and let rest for 30–60 minutes. (Everything up to this point can be done in advance.)

When you're ready to eat, make sure the tart is still a little warm (you can reheat it on the stove if need be) and place a plate on top. Carefully turn it over and lift the skillet off. Serve with some vanilla ice cream.

To drink: I think you're allowed to crack open the Calvados to go with this

96 Champagne sherbet

Homemade ice cream is a nightmare. I've tried making it myself and I've been served it at many friends' houses but although I'm always impressed by and grateful for all the effort, I have to admit that I've very rarely enjoyed it because the texture is somewhere between icy and slushy and rarely anywhere near creamy. Shockingly, the same goes for many restaurant-made ice creams.

Sherbets, however, are brilliant, reliable, and a little more forgiving, (although you really do need an ice cream maker for this). They are a blessed relief at lunch during a baking-hot summer, and they have a habit of bringing out the best in their ingredients. My favorites are elderflower and this Champagne one, which always gets people very excited when served. Your guests will always have a little space left for this.

Is Champagne too expensive to use for cooking?

You could use a really good sparkling wine to make this instead of Champagne, but flavors come through very clearly in a sherbet so don't use old or inferior wine. I once asked a chef, "Does it matter if you use inferior-quality wine for cooking?" The chef flew into a rage and started throwing things at me. The trouble is that when you cook with liquid ingredients, you tend to reduce them by evaporating the water in them, leaving behind the compounds that deliver the taste and flavor. So you don't lose or muddle flavors—you intensify them, and a bad wine will end up making the dish taste worse.

ingredients

Serves 4

juice of 1 lemon

$2^1/_4$ cups water

generous 1 cup sugar

1 tbsp liquid glucose

generous 1 cup Champagne

mint leaves or elderflower sprigs, to serve

To drink: More Champagne

method

Combine all the ingredients except the Champagne in a small saucepan. Place the pan over low heat and stir gently until all the sugar has dissolved. Increase the heat and bring to a boil, then remove from the heat. Let cool to room temperature.

Add the Champagne, pour into an ice cream maker and churn for 30–45 minutes, then serve.

Serve with a few mint leaves.

⑨⑦ Whole roasted pineapple

Pineapples have such a high level of sugar in their flesh that they caramelize when roasted, and this produces some of the most delectably sweet tastes of any food. This is a wonderfully rich and warming way to finish a meal. The best way to cook this is actually in an Indian clay tandoor oven, to make an extraordinary tandoori pineapple. It is spectacular.

I once managed to buy a whole bundle of ripe pineapples in Ethiopia, of all places. The flavor is entirely different when you eat ones that have ripened on the tree. It's a little like eating a tree-ripened mango. You bite into it, and the flavor dances out of the fruit and spreads throughout your head, overwhelming your olfactory bulb so that you think you've gone to fruit heaven.

What is a pineapple?

Well, it's not an apple, that's for sure. It's what's known as a "composite" or "multiple" fruit, made up of hundreds of fruitlets from little flowers that have fused together. The plants they grow from are short, around 3–5 feet/1–1.5 m tall. The word "pineapple" comes from their resemblance to pine cones, and they are often pollinated by hummingbirds (which, for some reason, makes me think they taste even nicer). You can tell a pineapple is ripe if you can easily pull a leaf out from the crown of the fruit. Pineapples contain an enzyme called bromelin that helps break down proteins, which is why pineapple is a powerful meat tenderizer and marinade ingredient. Use with care, or you might overcook your meat!

Pineapple carpaccio micro-recipe

I have to tell you about this absurdly easy and absurdly delicious pineapple dish. Simply take a pineapple and cut off all the skin, then slice it as thinly as you possibly can (if you are lucky enough to have an electric slicer for hams, use that). Mix 4 tablespoons of superfine sugar with 4 tablespoons of chopped fresh mint and beat together into a light green dust in a pestle and mortar. Lay out the pineapple slices on plates, edges overlapping, and sprinkle the minty sugar over the top. Serves 4 as a dessert.

To drink: An apple brandy liqueur

98 New York cheesecake

There are hundreds of different types of cheesecake around the world, and the dish has a long history, with one version cropping up as far back as the second century BC in Cato's *De Agri Cultura*. It has featured in many famous ancient cookery books (see opposite), throughout British and European literature, and there are important examples in Russia, India, and Italy too.

But anyone who claims that the United States isn't the world center of modern cheesecakery is kidding themselves. For my money, the New York cheesecake is the best of them all. It's an extraordinarily rich and creamy cooked version of the dish (although this recipe uses the ingenious British method of crushing graham crackers to make the base). It's by no means the world's most delicate or refined cheesecake (the French version is very light and the Japanese is so refined that it looks almost plastic), but by God it's good! Just remember that it tastes so much better if you make it the day before you plan to eat it.

Lindy's and Junior's

The original New York cheesecake recipe was popularized by Lindy's restaurant opened on Broadway by Leo "Lindy" Lindemann in 1921. Lindy's still sell cheesecakes, but Junior's deli, established since 1929, has come to rival its fame. In 1981, there was fire at the restaurant and a crowd of onlookers gathered chanting, "Save the Cheesecake."

To drink: A Grenache rosé

ingredients

Serves 10

generous ¹/₂ cup butter

5¹/₂ oz/150 g graham crackers, finely crushed

1 tbsp granulated sugar

2 lb/900 g cream cheese

1¹/₄ cups superfine sugar

2 tbsp all-purpose flour

1 tsp vanilla extract

finely grated zest of 1 orange

finely grated zest of 1 lemon

3 eggs

2 egg yolks

1¹/₄ cups heavy cream

The earliest English cheesecake

This is from the fourteenth-century cookbook *Forme of Cury* written by the chief Master Cooks of King Richard II of England.

TART DE BRY XX.VIII. VI.

Take a Crust ynche depe in a trape. take zolkes of Ayren rawe & chese ruayn. & medle it & be zolkes togyder. and do berto powdour gyngur. sugur. safroun. and salt. do it in a trape. bake it and serue it forth.

method

Preheat the oven to 350°F/180°C. Place a small saucepan over low heat, add the butter, and heat until it melts, then remove from the heat, stir in the crushed crackers and granulated sugar, and mix through. Press the cracker mixture tightly into the bottom of a 9-inch/23-cm springform cake pan. Place in the oven and bake for 10 minutes. Remove from the oven and let cool on a wire rack.

Increase the oven temperature to 400°F/200°C. With an electric food mixer beat the cheese until creamy, then gradually add the superfine sugar and flour and beat until smooth. Increase the speed and beat in the vanilla extract, orange zest, and lemon zest, then beat in the eggs and egg yolks one at a time. Finally, beat in the cream. Scrape any excess from the sides and paddles of the beater into the mixture. It should be light and whippy—beat on a faster setting if you need to.

Butter the sides of the cake pan and pour in the filling. Smooth the top, transfer to the preheated oven, and bake for 15 minutes, then reduce the temperature to 200°F/100°C and bake for an additional 30 minutes. Turn off the oven and let the cheesecake stand in it for 2 hours to cool and set. Cover and refrigerate overnight.

Slide a knife around the edge of the cake then unfasten the pan, cut the cheesecake into wedge-shaped slices, and serve.

⑨⑨ The world's finest cheeseboard

I'd hate to upset anyone here (and I know that cheese lovers are fiercely loyal to their local area) but I have eaten a vast and probably highly dangerous amount of cheese in my life, so I'm going to stick my neck out and suggest a list of the nine best cheeses available in the United States. These great cheeses are well worth seeking out.

The general consensus on cheeseboards is that you should start with mild cheeses, and work your way around them until you get to the strongest ones and, finally, the bleus. It's not a bad idea, as the stinkiest cheeses will make you less able to appreciate the subtle tastes of the more delicate offerings. In France, cheese will often be served after the main course and before a sweet dessert. In my house, I serve cheese last, and often I won't serve a dessert at all. That's because I just can't wait to get my hands on the stuff.

There's no golden number of cheeses to offer. I've chosen nine cheeses here because, well, it's my book and I like eating a lot of cheese, but you can have a marvelous cheesy experience with as few as three cheeses. In fact, my favorite cheese experience cropped up after eating a delicious Italian meal with my wife, when I asked if there was any cheese to finish with, but the waiter apologized and said "no." When he saw my crestfallen expression he said "Hang on a minute," and dashed into the kitchen, returning with the chef's entire round of Parmesan the size of the table. He gave me an oyster knife (one of the few tools able to crack a whole Parmesan) and left me to it. Ah, joy.

The mother of all cheeseboards

Nancy's Hudson Valley Camembert Made from cow's milk, this is creamy, soft-ripened, meltingly smooth and buttery cheese. As it ages its distinctive taste changes from mild to pungent. Hudson Valley, Vermont.

Constant Bliss A raw cow's milk cheese with a clean, creamy flavor overlaid with mushrooms. The distinctive yet mild taste contrasts beautifully with its hot, tangy rind. Greensboro, Vermont.

Humboldt Fog This moist goat cheese has a light texture and a wonderfully clean, lemony, goat's milk finish. McKinleyville, California.

Willow Hill Vermont Brebis A Camembert-style sheep cheese with a bloomy rind. Eat it as ripe as possible, when it has strong notes of earth and mushroom. Willow Hill Farm, Vermont.

Vintage Manchego I always think that properly aged, ancient Manchego, a hard sheep cheese, has an unmistakeable aroma of truffles. La Mancha, Spain.

Grayson A semi-soft warm and buttery cow's milk cheese that is tangy and fruity when young, but matures into a truly stinky cheese. Meadow Creek Farms, Virginia.

Keens Cheddar Not the strongest artisan cheddar around, but a good cheeseboard standby nonetheless. Made using unpasteurized cow's milk, it's soft and nutty but still delivers a powerful sour hit. Somerset, England.

Colston Bassett Stilton My Christmas favorite. A rich, blue-seamed cow's milk cheese, complex but not overpowering, and exceedingly creamy. Nottinghamshire, England.

Epoisses For the complete stinker medal, it's a toss up between this and Stinking Bishop, but as my four-year-old daughter Daisy reckons this is her favorite, I'll go with her. This is a strong, aromatic and animal-ey washed-rind cow's milk cheese. Catch it just before it goes over the taste threshold and develops a manure aroma. Burgundy, France

To accompany the cheeses:

Quince paste (a thick, orangey-brown jam of quince pears that accompanies strong, hard cheese, especially Manchego)

Medjool dates (fat, plump sweet dates)

Cold grapes straight from the refrigerator

The thinnest crackers money can buy

Thin slices of apple (to put cheese on in place of crackers)

To drink: I love eating cheese with red wines, and although it may seem a little unfashionable these days, I love a good vintage port

⑩ Panettone bread-and-butter pudding

French toast

It's sometimes said that the British bread-and-butter pudding is a baked version of French toast, although I'd contend that that's a little like saying that the world's finest Pata Negra Spanish ham (see page 80) is a dried version of meat loaf. Nonetheless, French toast is also a pretty good way to enjoy simple ingredients like bread and egg. In my house we call this fairy bread or gypsy bread, and I make it simply by mixing eggs with a little milk, then putting bread slices into the mixture until it is all soaked up. The slices are then fried in butter and served with a little honey. It's easy to make and it's good stuff, especially for a breakfast that's just a cut above the usual.

I used to think that bread-and-butter pudding was one of those classic inviolable recipes that were protected from infringement, adaptation, or development by some strict Global Bread-and-Butter Recipe Security Agency. I mean, how much better can a dessert get?

Then I met my future wife. And shortly after meeting her, I met her bread and butter pudding recipe made with panettone—and then my culinary understanding fell apart. And shortly after that, I met her bread and butter pudding recipe made with chocolate panettone, and my life burst into a myriad culinary fragments, only to be put back together by her. I'm not overdoing this am I?

Bread and butter pudding is a lightly spiced "cake" of bread baked after soaking in a divine vanilla-ed custard. It's immensely popular in Britain—on a par with Sticky Toffee Pudding—and it's a school and nursery classic that has found its way onto the menus of some of the finest restaurants in the world.

This is a great recipe to make after Christmas, when there are a lot of huge Italian panettone breads knocking around, but do watch out for the levels of vanilla—if the panettone is already well-spiced, adding more can make it overpowering.

ingredients

Serves 4–6

scant 1 cup raisins, golden raisins, or chopped dates

4 tbsp brandy

1 1/4 cups milk

scant 2 cups heavy cream

1 vanilla bean, split, or 1 tsp vanilla extract

scant 3/4 cup butter, softened, plus extra for greasing

10 medium loaf-sized slices of panettone, preferably chocolate-flavored, or white bread, crusts removed

4 eggs

3/4 cup superfine sugar

vanilla ice cream, to serve

method

Put the raisins in a bowl with the brandy and let soften for an hour or two. In a small saucepan, warm (but don't boil) the milk and cream and add the split vanilla bean. Let stand for 30 minutes.

Preheat the oven to 350°F/180°C. Butter a shallow ovenproof dish. Butter the panettone slices, cut them diagonally in half, and lay in an overlapping pattern in the dish. Remove the softened raisins from the brandy, reserving the brandy, and sprinkle them over the pannetone.

In a large bowl, whisk the eggs with the sugar. Remove the vanilla bean from the milk and discard, and add the cream and milk to the egg mixture. Add the reserved brandy and whisk. Pour this mixture over the panettone and press the slices down so that they soak in the custard. Make sure that the edges don't stick out too far above the surface of the custard.

Transfer to the preheated oven and bake for 30–40 minutes, until the custard has dried and set golden brown but before the pannetone burns. Serve hot, with vanilla ice cream.

To drink: Pineau des Charentes—an aperitif, really, made from unfermented grape must and Cognac

101st dish
Fugu fish
WARNING!

I toyed with all the amazing tastes and flavors, textures, and sensory overloads, the extraordinary experiences, and the moral and emotional journeys that food has taken me on. But in the end there really was only one dish worthy of ending this book. It's the most dramatic of all culinary experiences, a climax of both cuisine, crisis, and nonsense all at once: Fugu, the deadly puffer fish whose liver is 1,000 times more poisonous than cyanide. Estimated annual fugu fatalities range from 0–6 (if you believe the Tokyo Bureau of Social Welfare and Health) to as many as 100 per year (if you believe the more anecdotal reports).

In Japan, fugu is also a revered delicacy, served only in special restaurants where the chef has passed an exam qualifying him to prepare it. It's expensive, too.

I ate fugu in Tokyo, having seen a tank of fugu bobbing haplessly in a restaurant window. My chef had a special license—I know this because I went into his kitchen and asked him to show me, although considering that I don't speak Japanese, he could have been showing me his bus pass. He explained what would happen if he poisoned me: My tongue would be paralyzed and I would begin to suffocate. At this point, I stepped outside to phone my wife who was back home in London with my newborn daughter. She knew that I lived for culinary adventure, but I needed to consult her before doing something potentially deadly. The phone rang. Voice mail. Damn, I was on my own.

So what is fugu like? Well, I ate it as a soup, with fugu fin floating in it, followed by fugu sashimi. My chef seemed nervous and hesitant, thereby adding to the tension. I drank the soup first, a delicate, clean fishy broth with croutons of salty, crunchy fins. It made me sweat and palpitate—whether from fugu poisoning or damp heat, I knew not. Then the centerpiece: The sashimi. It was cut so thin that the plate was visible through it, and it tasted like finest sea bass—clean, pure, with the lightest, tiniest hint of fishiness. If I weren't so excited I'd say it was almost blandly clean, but my heart was racing, my mind was in a tumble, and my mouth and tongue began to tingle. I don't know whether this was the legendary fugu sensation (supposedly from traces of the neurotoxin) or simply the psychological climax I was going through. Either way, I loved every second of it, my mind focused on my mouth and stomach like never before.

Now that's what I call a memorable dinner.

So what's the point?

Some people (myself included) believe that eating is not just about flavor and taste but a combination of sensations and emotions, and that sound, touch, fear, drama, and love all have a tangible effect on the experience of eating, sometimes transcending calorific value and becoming excitement, revelation, or joy. I know that some people dismiss this as a load of old nonsense and see theater in food as in some way immoral, but I bet they love a birthday cake, a wedding cake, or a plateau de fruits de mer when it arrives with a flourish. Anyone who isn't excited by the pop of a Champagne cork, the serving of a suckling pig, a grand aïoli, or even a tacky parfait ice cream is no friend of mine.

To drink: Vintage sake from highly polished rice. And lots of it

Why is fugu so special?

The puffer fish is a poor swimmer. Its tail is too short, its body too fat. It is painfully slow, and seems to have little control over its direction or altitude, and it fairly waddles and wobbles through the water. If you were its fishy friend, you'd be embarrassed to be seen out with it, if it weren't for the fact that it has an extraordinary ability to puff up into a vicious ball of spikes at the drop of a fin and it has extremely high levels of a toxin called tetrodoxin in its liver, ovaries, and skin, which shuts down the nerve signaling, causing paralysis and death by asphyxiation. There is no known antidote and fugu rates as the second most poisonous animal in the world (after the golden poison frog).

INDEX